EMOTIONAL DETACHMENT

Workbook For Personal Transformation And Self-Help

EVELYN T. AVERY

ALL RIGHTS RESERVED

Editorial Reviews

"This workbook is a beacon of hope for anyone striving to break free from emotional entanglements and embrace their truest selves. The author's ability to weave professional insight with relatable life scenarios makes this a must-read for anyone on a healing journey. Every chapter is filled with practical tools that feel as though they were written just for you."
— Dr. Sandra Colls, *Licensed Therapist and Trauma Specialist*

"The depth of understanding displayed in this book is a proof of the author's dedication to empowering her readers. Her previous works have always left a lasting impression, but this workbook truly stands out as a guide for sailing through the complexities of emotional detachment with compassion and clarity."
— John A. Peterson, Editor-in-Chief, *Empowerment Books Publishing*

"As a proofreader, I was captivated not just by the author's mastery of language but by the heartfelt approach to such a nuanced topic. This is more than a book—it's a transformative experience designed to guide readers toward emotional freedom and resilience."
— Jessica B. Reeves, *Professional Proofreader*

"Rarely does a book resonate so deeply with readers of all backgrounds. The author's ability to connect theoretical

insights with practical applications is unparalleled. It's evident that her years of experience have culminated in this remarkable guide."
— Maria Davidson, *Co-Author and Mental Health Advocate*

"This workbook is a gift to anyone seeking clarity and balance in their emotional lives. The exercises are simple yet profound, the reflections are deeply personal, and the overall tone is one of encouragement and hope. It is a proof of the author's passion for guiding others toward self-discovery."
— Dr. E.D. Foster, *Clinical Psychologist*

"Having collaborated with the author on some of her previous projects, I can confidently say her work is always infused with authenticity and a genuine desire to help. This book is no exception. It takes readers by the hand and leads them to a place of empowerment and peace."
— Michael T. Benson, *Co-Author and Relationship Coach*

"The relatability of the content makes this workbook an invaluable tool for both professionals and individuals navigating the roads of emotional challenges. The practical questions are relatable, making it easy to apply the lessons to daily life."
— Sarah Julius Ben, *Editor*

"The author has once again proven her ability to write in a way that speaks directly to the heart. Every chapter feels like a conversation with a trusted friend who truly understands your struggles and offers gentle yet firm guidance forward."
— Rachel W. Stone, *Proofreader*

"This workbook is not just about emotional detachment.

 It's more about reclaiming your power and finding true peace. The author's unique ability to combine professional expertise with her personal understanding makes this a standout resource in the self-help genre."
— Dr. Kevin H. John, *Psychiatrist and Trauma Recovery Specialist*

"As someone who has edited numerous self-help books, I can confidently say that this book is among the most impactful works I've had the pleasure to review. The author's voice is compassionate and relatable, and her strategies are both actionable and transformative. For anyone reading this right now, just get a copy of this masterpiece and thank me later."
— Megan C. Parcker, *Senior Editor, Wellness Horizons Press*

"What sets this workbook apart is the author's ability to translate complex psychological concepts into accessible, meaningful tools. Her words inspire readers to reflect, grow, and take control of their emotional well-being. It's a privilege to recommend this book."
— Davidson Mcwell, *Co-Author*

"This book feels like a lifeline to those seeking emotional balance. The content is relatable, the exercises are practical, and the message is one of hope and empowerment. The author's commitment to helping others shines through on every page."
— Anabel Ramire, *Proofreader and Wellness Advocate*

TABLE OF CONTENTS

DEDICATION

This book is dedicated to those who have struggled in silence, carrying emotional burdens too heavy to bear, yet too familiar to release. To the ones who have felt trapped in the cycles of pain, seeking a way to reclaim their peace and freedom—you are not alone, and your courage to seek change is a profound act of strength.

To every soul navigating the complexities of relationships, self-discovery, and healing, this book is a testament to your resilience and a guide to help you find the clarity and balance you deserve.

To my readers, may this journey of emotional detachment open doors to healing, self-awareness, and the inner peace you've long sought. And to those who supported this vision, your encouragement and belief in this work have been my unwavering light. Thank you for walking alongside me in this purpose-driven endeavor.

ACKNOWLEDGEMENTS

The creation of this book has been a profoundly meaningful and enlightening journey, made possible by the unwavering support, wisdom, and dedication of many extraordinary individuals who have touched my life throughout this process.

To everyone who has embarked on their own journey of emotional detachment and shared their stories of triumph, vulnerability, and growth, your courage has been the foundation of this work. Your willingness to reflect on and transcend life's most challenging moments has been a source of endless inspiration.

I am deeply grateful to my family and friends, who stood steadfastly by my side, offering love, understanding, and encouragement even when the path felt uncertain. Your presence and belief in this vision sustained me through the most demanding stages of this endeavor.

To the experts, mentors, and colleagues who generously shared their knowledge and insights in psychology, mindfulness, and emotional well-being, thank you for shaping this book with your invaluable expertise. Your contributions ensured this work remains practical, thoughtful, and deeply rooted in the understanding of human emotions.

A heartfelt thanks to my editor, whose precision and dedication have been instrumental in refining this book into something I hope will serve as a meaningful guide to its readers. Your careful guidance and commitment to excellence have brought clarity and resonance to these pages.

To every reader who chooses to explore these ideas, thank you for your trust and willingness to prioritize your emotional well-being. This book was written with the hope that it will serve as a steadfast companion on your path to healing, self-discovery, and empowerment.

May this book be a reminder that emotional detachment does not mean disconnection but rather the embrace of freedom, peace, and the courage to honor one's emotional space with clarity and grace.

WHY THIS BOOK?

Life often presents us with emotional challenges that leave us feeling overwhelmed, disconnected, or trapped in patterns that no longer serve us. Whether it's the lingering pain of past relationships, the strain of unmet expectations, or the heavy burden of emotional overcommitment, finding a way to reclaim peace and clarity can feel like an uphill battle. This guide is for everyone and anyone seeking not just relief but transformation—a way to redefine the relationship with their emotions and create a life rooted in balance, freedom, and inner strength.

This book isn't about avoidance or apathy. It's about empowerment. Emotional detachment, as explored here, isn't the shutting off of emotions but the cultivation of a healthier connection to them. It's learning to respond rather than react, to protect your boundaries without guilt, and to nurture relationships without losing your individuality.

What sets this guide apart is its holistic approach to emotional detachment. With a blend of practical strategies, it provides a roadmap for personal growth that is both actionable and profound. It guides you through understanding your emotional triggers, building resilience, setting and maintaining boundaries, and creating meaningful connections—all while prioritizing your mental and emotional well-being.

This is more than just a guide—it's a handy tool for transformation. It speaks to those who are ready to let go of emotional entanglements that hinder their growth, embrace the power of intentional self-care, and find peace in every facet of their lives. Whether you're just beginning your journey or seeking to deepen your understanding, this handbook offers the insights and handy tools to foster a profound shift in how you approach your emotions and relationships.

For anyone ready to step into a life of clarity, authenticity, and empowerment, this hand book serves as a compassionate companion, offering guidance and support every step of the way.

CHECK OUT THE AUTHOR'S OTHER BOOKS LISTED TOWARDS THE END OF THIS BOOK

WHAT TO EXPECT FROM THIS BOOK

1. **Personal Experience And Professional Insight:** This book is born from a deep understanding of the emotional struggles that many face. It combines real-world experiences with professional insights into emotional detachment, offering a perspective that is both compassionate and relatable. Through careful exploration of personal anecdotes and psychological expertise, it bridges the gap between understanding emotions and managing them effectively.

2. **Comprehensive Approach:** Every chapter of this guide takes you through a journey of emotional awareness, resilience, and transformation. It doesn't merely skim the surface but goes deep into essential aspects like mindfulness, self-care, boundary setting, and emotional intelligence. This book is a holistic resource, addressing every layer of emotional detachment to help you achieve balance and freedom.

3. **Practical Tools And Exercises:** Understanding is only the beginning. This guide is filled with actionable strategies, thought-provoking self-reflective questions, and transformative exercises that encourage growth. Each tool is designed to empower you to take charge of your emotional well-being and apply these concepts to your daily life.

4. **Empowerment And Hope:** Emotional detachment isn't about shutting down feelings; it's about creating space for self-discovery, healing, and growth. This book is written with the belief that every individual has the power to reshape their

emotional landscape. It inspires hope, offering guidance that leads to clarity, strength, and the courage to let go of what no longer serves you.

5. **Accessibility And Usability:** Whether you're new to the concept of emotional detachment or seeking to deepen your practice, this book is crafted to meet you where you are. Its clear language, structured format, and step-by-step guides make it a resource that is both easy to understand and highly effective, ensuring that every reader like you, can benefit from its insights.

NOTE: The benefits of this invaluable tool extend beyond the gains listed above—there is much more to discover within this book.

CHECK PAGE 154 TO GET YOUR FREE GIFT

HOW TO USE THIS GUIDE

This book is designed as an interactive guide to assist you on your journey toward emotional detachment and personal growth. Its structure allows you to engage deeply with the material while tailoring the lessons to your unique experiences and needs. To make the most of this resource, we encourage you to approach it with openness, curiosity, and a willingness to reflect.

As you move through the chapters, you will encounter a series of **"self-reflective questions"**. These questions are crafted to guide you toward a deeper understanding of your emotions, behaviors, and thought patterns. Take the time to read each question thoughtfully and jot down your genuine responses in the spaces provided or in a personal journal. Your answers will serve as a mirror, reflecting areas that require attention, growth, or change. Through this process, you will uncover insights about what you need to embrace, learn, or let go of to achieve the emotional freedom you seek.

Additionally, the book includes practical exercises, strategies, and tools designed to reinforce the concepts explored. These activities are meant to be actionable, helping you integrate the lessons into your daily life. Whether it's practicing mindfulness techniques, setting boundaries, or exploring self-care rituals, each exercise is an opportunity to apply what you'll learn and witness the transformative impact it can have.

To optimize your experience:

- Dedicate uninterrupted time to each chapter and exercise, allowing yourself the space to fully engage.
- Be honest and forthcoming in your reflections—this book is a judgment-free zone, intended to foster personal growth.
- Revisit sections as needed, especially if certain concepts resonate with you more deeply at different stages of your journey.

Above all, remember that this book is a partnership in your quest for inner peace and freedom. Trust the process, embrace the challenges, and celebrate the progress you make along the way. This is your journey, and every step forward brings you closer to the clarity and empowerment you deserve.

INTRODUCTION

John met Mariam during his second year of college. She was the type of person who could light up a room with her infectious laughter and warm smile. They bonded over late-night study sessions, shared playlists, and their mutual love for philosophy. Over time, their friendship blossomed into a deep, unconditional love. They became inseparable, a team determined to build a future together. But beneath Mariam's bright exterior lay a silent struggle that John only began to notice as their relationship grew more intimate.

Mariam was emotionally distant at times, shutting down during arguments or retreating into herself when overwhelmed. John, though deeply in love, often felt as though he was grasping at smoke, trying to connect with someone who always seemed just out of reach. Mariam, on the other hand, didn't understand why she felt so disconnected, at first. It wasn't that she didn't love John; she simply didn't know how to let him into the very parts of her heart she had guarded for so long.

Their first year of marriage brought these struggles to the forefront. Mariam's tendency to avoid vulnerability clashed with John's yearning for emotional closeness. The moments of joy they shared were overshadowed by an unspoken tension that neither could fully articulate. Mariam often found herself pulling away, fearing that revealing her fears and insecurities would make her appear weak. John, frustrated and hurt, began questioning whether they were truly compatible.

One evening, after a particularly heated argument about Mariam's reluctance to discuss her feelings, she broke down in tears and admitted, "<u>I don't know how to do this. I don't know how to open up</u>." John, though hurt, wrapped her in his loving arms and whispered, "<u>Then we'll figure it out together</u>."

Determined to save their marriage and their future, Mariam decided to seek therapy. Her therapist helped her uncover the roots of her emotional detachment, tracing it back to her childhood where vulnerability was often met with rejection. In the process, Mariam was faced with lots of bad experiences, pains, and grief of her childhood. The therapist recommended a book that had helped many of her clients in the past: a guide on emotional detachment and healing. Initially Mariam was skeptical, but she later agreed to give it a chance, and also invited John to read it with her.

The book became their lifeline. Together, they explored its pages, which were filled with relatable stories, practical exercises, and insights that spoke directly to their struggles. The book encouraged them to journal their emotions, reflect on their triggers, and engage in activities that fostered trust and vulnerability. It taught them the importance of emotional awareness and provided step-by-step guidance for reconnecting with themselves and each other.

One exercise asked them to write letters to their younger selves, addressing the fears and insecurities they had carried into adulthood. Mariam's letter revealed her fear of abandonment and rejection, while John's letter expressed his anxiety about never being "enough." Sharing these letters with each other was a transformative experience. For the first time, Mariam allowed John to see the depth of her pain, and John responded not with judgment but with understanding and compassion.

Another chapter in the book focused on creating safe spaces for honest communication. They learned how to listen without interrupting, how to express their needs using "I" statements, and how to validate each other's feelings. Mariam practiced saying, "*I feel overwhelmed when...*" instead of shutting down, while John learned to say, "*I hear you, and I'm here for you,*" instead of trying to fix her emotions.

Over a few months of applying the book's principles, their relationship began to shift. Mariam's walls slowly crumbled, allowing John to see the vulnerable and authentic woman he had fallen in love with. John, in turn, became more patient and supportive, celebrating Mariam's progress while working on his own emotional awareness.

The turning point came one evening when Mariam, without prompting, opened up about a childhood memory that had haunted her for years. It was a moment of raw honesty that left them both in tears, but it also brought a profound sense of connection. "I trust you," she said softly, and John knew that those three words put together carried more weight than any declaration of love.

Their journey wasn't without setbacks. There were moments of doubt, frustration, and fear. But they faced each challenge with the tools they had learned, leaning on each other and the wisdom of the book. They discovered that healing was not a linear process but a series of steps forward and backward, all leading to growth and understanding.

Years later, as they celebrated their fifth wedding anniversary, John looked at Mariam with a mix of admiration and gratitude. She was no longer the guarded college girl he had fallen in love with but a woman who had embraced her emotional depth and allowed him to do the same. Their marriage, once fragile, had become a sanctuary built on trust, vulnerability, and mutual growth. Reflecting on their journey, Mariam said, "That book didn't just save our marriage; it helped me find myself." John smiled, holding her hand tightly, knowing that their shared journey had been the greatest adventure of his life yet.

So, like many others, you wear a mask, a carefully crafted facade that hides your true self from the world. Behind this mask, your emotions are suppressed, your vulnerabilities concealed. While this mask may protect you from pain, it also prevents you from experiencing the full spectrum of human emotion. By embracing emotional awareness and authenticity, you can shed this mask and reveal your true self to the world. You can learn to feel your emotions deeply, without fear or judgment. This journey of self-discovery will empower you to build stronger relationships with the right people, achieve your goals, and live a more fulfilling life.

Join me as we step together into a deeper understanding of what it means to embrace emotional freedom and create lasting change.

Chapter 1

Overview Of Emotional Detachment

{Personal Transformation & Self-Help Journey}

Understanding Emotional Detachment

Emotional detachment is often misunderstood, mischaracterized as a lack of care or empathy. In reality, it is a skill that allows individuals to experience a sense of emotional clarity and control in their lives. It is neither about suppressing feelings nor about disengaging from the world; instead, it fosters the ability to observe emotions without being controlled by them. Emotional detachment empowers individuals to make choices rooted in rationality and purpose, rather than reactionary impulses driven by heightened emotional states.

At its core, emotional detachment is an intentional practice. It involves cultivating a balanced relationship with emotions, where one neither denies nor becomes consumed by them. This balance requires awareness of feelings as they arise and the wisdom to respond with calm and thoughtful action. Far from being cold or unfeeling, this approach brings depth to personal interactions, enabling a more authentic and compassionate connection with others while maintaining one's inner stability.

One of the most significant misconceptions about emotional detachment is the belief that it equates to emotional numbness. Some assume it involves shutting off emotions entirely to avoid pain or discomfort. However, this may not be far from the truth. Emotional detachment does not advocate for avoidance; rather, it promotes understanding and acknowledgment. By recognizing emotions as fleeting experiences rather than permanent states, individuals can avoid being overwhelmed by their intensity.

Another fallacy tied to emotional detachment is the idea that it fosters disconnection from others. Critics often misinterpret it as a barrier to meaningful relationships. On the contrary, emotional detachment enhances relational dynamics by preventing unnecessary conflicts and misunderstandings. When one is no longer trapped in reactive emotional loops, they can approach conversations and conflicts with composure, fostering an environment of trust and open communication.

The role of emotional detachment in personal growth cannot be overstated. At its essence, it is a tool for self-mastery. Life is filled with stressors and challenges, many of which are beyond individual control. Without a framework for managing emotions, it's easy to become consumed by frustration, anxiety, or despair. Emotional detachment acts as a buffer, allowing one to observe these stressors without becoming entangled in their emotional weight. This detachment leads to a more measured perspective, reducing the mental clutter that often accompanies reactive thinking.

Clarity is another gift offered by emotional detachment. When emotions are unchecked, they can cloud judgment and lead to impulsive decisions that do not align with long-term goals or values. Emotional detachment encourages individuals to pause, reflect, and evaluate situations objectively. This clarity brings about a sense of empowerment, as individuals learn to trust their ability to handle life's complexities without being overwhelmed.

For those on a journey toward greater mental clarity, emotional detachment offers a pathway to freedom. It challenges the narrative that emotions must dictate actions and decisions. Instead, it invites individuals to reframe their relationship with emotions, viewing them as signals rather than directives. For example, anger might signal a boundary violation, but it does not necessitate retaliation. By acknowledging the emotion without succumbing to it, you can retain your agency and control.

In the realm of personal transformation, emotional detachment serves as a bridge to greater self-awareness. It teaches individuals to identify emotional patterns that may have unconsciously governed their lives. These patterns, often rooted in past experiences, can distort perceptions of the present. Emotional detachment helps to disentangle the past from the present, offering the opportunity to respond authentically rather than react habitually.

This practice is particularly powerful in fostering resilience. Life's inevitable challenges test emotional stability, and without a method for processing these experiences, they can lead to burnout or prolonged distress. Emotional detachment provides the mental space needed to regroup and recover. It fosters a mindset where challenges are seen not as insurmountable crises but as opportunities for growth and learning.

Cultivating emotional detachment also redefines the concept of control. Many individuals fall into the trap of believing they must control every aspect of their lives to achieve happiness. This belief often leads to frustration when faced with the unpredictability of life. Emotional detachment shifts the focus from controlling external circumstances to managing one's internal response. It emphasizes that while one cannot dictate the behavior of others or prevent every difficulty, they can choose how to respond to these challenges.

This shift in focus also enhances interpersonal relationships. Emotional detachment allows individuals to approach relationships from a place of wholeness rather than dependency. It encourages a mindset where love and care are given freely, without expectations of reciprocity. This perspective reduces feelings of disappointment or resentment when others do not meet one's expectations, creating space for more genuine and fulfilling connections.

Implementing emotional detachment requires intentional effort and practice. It begins with self-awareness—developing the ability to recognize when emotions are influencing thoughts and actions. Practices such as mindfulness, journaling, and reflective exercises can help you build this awareness. Once emotions are identified, the next step is acceptance. This involves allowing emotions to exist without judgment, understanding that they are temporary states rather than permanent fixtures.

Detachment also involves the cultivation of new thought patterns. Instead of dwelling on what cannot be changed, emotionally detached individuals focus on what they can control—their reactions, attitudes, and decisions. This shift from external to internal focus reduces feelings of helplessness and enhances a sense of personal power.

For those concerned about losing their emotional depth, it's important to emphasize that emotional detachment does not diminish one's ability to feel deeply. Instead, it creates a framework where emotions are felt fully but do not overpower. This balance allows individuals to experience the richness of life's emotions—joy, sorrow, love, and even pain—without becoming trapped by them.

Emotional detachment is not about perfection. There will be moments when emotions are overwhelming or when old patterns resurface. The key lies in approaching these moments with compassion and a willingness to learn. Every setback is an opportunity to deepen the practice of detachment and reinforce its benefits.

Ultimately, emotional detachment is a practice of liberation. It frees individuals from the chains of reactive living, offering the clarity and strength needed to navigate life's complexities. It is not about avoiding the storms of life but about finding the calm within them. By embracing emotional detachment, individuals open the door to a life of greater peace, resilience, and authenticity.

The Benefits of Emotional Detachment for Self-Help and Transformation

Emotional detachment is a transformative approach that cultivates clarity, stability, and growth in life's complexities. It fosters a sense of resilience that is essential for overcoming the inevitable challenges and uncertainties we face. Far from being an act of disconnection, it encourages a thoughtful engagement with oneself and others, reducing emotional strain and paving the way for healthier, more fulfilling relationships and decisions.

Resilience, the ability to recover and adapt after setbacks, is one of the most significant benefits of emotional detachment. Life often presents situations that are beyond our control, from personal conflicts to unforeseen challenges. Emotional detachment empowers individuals to face such moments with composure. By creating a mental buffer, it enables a person to step back and evaluate a situation without being consumed by its emotional weight. This separation does not signify avoidance but rather a strategic pause that allows for reflection and thoughtful response.

In reducing emotional overwhelm, emotional detachment acts as a grounding force. Overwhelming emotions often cloud judgment and lead to reactive behaviors that do not align with long-term goals or values. For example, anger, unchecked, might escalate a disagreement into unnecessary conflict. Through detachment, individuals can observe these feelings without becoming entangled, fostering a calm state of mind that supports constructive action.

This clarity is particularly valuable when managing stress, a pervasive element of modern life. Stress often stems from over-identification with external circumstances or the relentless need for control. Emotional detachment reframes this relationship, emphasizing the importance of focusing on one's internal state rather than external outcomes. As a result, individuals experience a reduction in mental clutter, allowing them to prioritize what truly matters and let go of what does not.

In interpersonal relationships, emotional detachment supports the cultivation of healthier dynamics. It discourages co-dependency and over-reliance on others for validation or fulfillment. Instead, it promotes an approach rooted in mutual respect and autonomy. Relationships become more balanced when individuals are not overly influenced by their own or others' emotional fluctuations. This fosters an environment where connections thrive on trust, understanding, and genuine care, free from the distortions of unchecked emotions.

Detachment also enhances communication. When emotions are regulated, conversations become clearer, and intentions are better understood. For instance, during a disagreement, a detached mindset allows one to focus on the issue at hand rather than reacting defensively. This objectivity reduces miscommunication and strengthens the foundation of relationships, whether personal or professional.

Another significant advantage lies in decision-making. Emotions, though valuable, can sometimes lead to impulsive choices that may not serve long-term goals. Detachment offers a framework for evaluating decisions objectively, ensuring that actions align with values and priorities rather than being dictated by transient feelings. Whether deciding on a career move, resolving a conflict, or making daily life choices, emotional detachment provides the clarity needed to act with confidence and purpose.

One way emotional detachment supports better decisions is by minimizing the influence of external pressures. The opinions and expectations of others often weigh heavily on personal choices. Detachment encourages individuals to honor their authenticity by prioritizing what feels right to them rather than succumbing to societal or relational pressures. This strengthens one's sense of self and builds a life that reflects personal values and aspirations.

Additionally, emotional detachment helps individuals set and maintain boundaries. Boundaries are essential for preserving mental and emotional health, yet they can be challenging to establish when emotions dominate. Detachment provides the clarity and strength needed to recognize when boundaries are necessary and to communicate them assertively without guilt or fear.

The transformative power of emotional detachment also lies in its ability to shift perspectives. By encouraging a broader view of situations, it prevents over-identification with challenges or difficulties. This mental flexibility allows individuals to see opportunities for growth and learning even in adversity. Detachment does not diminish the significance of life's events but places them in a context that supports personal development rather than emotional entrapment.

Furthermore, emotional detachment fosters inner peace. When the need to control external circumstances diminishes, a sense of freedom emerges. This freedom allows individuals to focus on their personal growth and well-being, creating space for joy, creativity, and fulfillment. It is not about detaching from life but engaging with it more fully, with a sense of stability and clarity that enhances every experience.

The path to emotional detachment is not about rejecting emotions but embracing them with a mindful awareness. It involves understanding that emotions are temporary states, not definitive truths. This perspective reduces the power of negative emotions, such as fear, jealousy, or regret, while enhancing positive emotions like gratitude and contentment.

By fostering resilience, emotional detachment strengthens the ability to cope with life's ups and downs. It instills a sense of confidence in one's capacity to handle challenges without being overwhelmed. This self-assurance creates a foundation for exploring new possibilities and embracing change, essential elements of personal transformation.

In relationships, detachment allows individuals to give and receive love more freely. By releasing expectations and demands, it nurtures connections based on authenticity and mutual respect. This approach enhances intimacy, as it removes the emotional barriers that often hinder closeness.

Decision-making benefits greatly from the practice of detachment. Choices made with a detached mindset are more likely to reflect long-term priorities and values. This approach reduces the risk of regret and supports a life aligned with personal goals and aspirations.

In sum, emotional detachment offers a pathway to a life of greater clarity, stability, and fulfillment. It is a skill that can be developed with practice and intention, providing profound benefits for self-help and transformation. By reducing emotional overwhelm, fostering healthy relationships, and enhancing decision-making, it equips individuals with the tools to navigate life's complexities with confidence and grace. It is not about escaping emotions but understanding and engaging with them in a way that supports growth, resilience, and inner peace.

Chapter 2

Emotional Awareness

{Understanding & Acknowledging Emotion}

The Importance of Recognizing Your Emotions

Emotions are an inherent part of the human experience, intricately woven into the fabric of our daily lives. They serve as signals, guiding us through decisions, relationships, and personal growth. At their essence, emotions are the body's way of interpreting and responding to internal and external stimuli. They provide a language through which our mind and body communicate, shaping how we perceive and interact with the world. Rather than being distractions or nuisances, emotions are tools for self-discovery, alerting us to our needs, boundaries, and desires.

The role of emotions in personal growth is profound. They reflect our inner state and can be seen as indicators of areas that require attention or change. Joy, for instance, shows alignment with our values or desires, while discomfort or sadness might suggest unmet needs or unresolved issues. Recognizing these signals is not just about understanding what we feel in a given moment but about identifying patterns and tendencies that influence our behavior and choices. When emotions are acknowledged and processed effectively, they become a gateway to deeper self-awareness and intentional living.

Ignoring or suppressing emotions, however, can have significant repercussions on both mental and physical health. The mind and body are interconnected systems, and emotional neglect often manifests as psychological or physiological distress. Suppressed feelings do not disappear; instead, they accumulate, sometimes re-emerging as anxiety, irritability, or feelings of emptiness. Over time, unresolved emotions can lead to chronic stress, a condition that weakens the immune system, disrupts sleep patterns, and increases vulnerability to illnesses. Physically, the body may exhibit signs of emotional suppression through tension, fatigue, or unexplained aches, all of which are often overlooked as mere inconveniences.

On a mental level, ignoring emotions can create a disconnect from one's sense of self. When feelings are dismissed, the ability to identify personal needs and boundaries becomes impaired, resulting in confusion and a lack of direction. Emotional suppression also limits the capacity for authentic connections with others, as unprocessed feelings may create barriers to trust and understanding. This disconnection can foster isolation, even in the midst of social interactions, leading to a sense of being misunderstood or unseen.

Common signs of emotional disconnection can manifest in subtle yet pervasive ways. One of the most recognizable indicators is a constant state of emotional numbness, where individuals find it challenging to experience joy, sadness, or any other emotion with intensity. This emotional flatness often coincides with a lack of enthusiasm for activities that once brought satisfaction, leading to a diminished quality of life.

Another frequent sign is difficulty identifying or articulating feelings. Some people may find themselves unable to pinpoint why they feel unsettled, instead brushing it off as a vague sense of unease. This difficulty often extends to interactions with others, where expressing vulnerability or engaging in meaningful conversations feels foreign or uncomfortable. The inability to name emotions not only stifles personal growth but also inhibits relational intimacy.

Physical symptoms also provide clues about emotional disconnection. Chronic tension, particularly in areas such as the neck, shoulders, or jaw, can signal suppressed stress or frustration. Similarly, digestive issues like nausea or stomach aches may point to unacknowledged anxiety. These symptoms persist because the body, unable to release the emotional energy through healthy outlets, channels it into physical manifestations.

Behavioral patterns also reveal the effects of emotional disconnection. Avoidance becomes a common coping mechanism, whether through constant busyness, excessive consumption of media, or substance use. These distractions serve to suppress awareness of underlying emotions, creating a temporary sense of relief while deepening the disconnection over time. People in this state often find themselves reacting impulsively or disproportionately to minor irritations, as unresolved emotions resurface in unpredictable ways.

One particularly insidious effect of ignoring emotions is the tendency to over-rely on external validation. Without a strong connection to one's inner emotional world, individuals often seek affirmation from others to fill the void. This reliance not only places an unsustainable burden on relationships but also leaves individuals vulnerable to manipulation and disappointment. A lack of emotional awareness weakens the foundation of self-trust, making it difficult to discern genuine needs from external expectations.

The importance of recognizing emotions lies not in avoiding discomfort but in embracing the full spectrum of human experience. Emotions, whether positive or challenging, provide insights into what truly matters. By identifying and accepting these feelings, you can begin the process of healing and transformation. The act of recognition itself is a powerful step toward breaking cycles of suppression and self-neglect.

A key aspect of emotional awareness is learning to view emotions as transient. Understanding that feelings are not permanent but rather fleeting experiences allows individuals to engage with them without fear or resistance. This perspective creates space for constructive responses rather than reactive behaviors, fostering a sense of empowerment and control.

Ultimately, emotional awareness is not merely about acknowledging emotions but about using them as a compass for personal growth. When feelings are understood and processed, they reveal deeper truths about values, aspirations, and areas of potential change. This understanding fosters a life of greater alignment, where choices are guided by authenticity rather than external pressures or unresolved pain.

Recognizing emotions is not an innate skill but a practice that develops over time. It requires patience and a willingness to confront the discomfort of unprocessed feelings. The rewards, however, are transformative, offering a renewed sense of clarity, connection, and purpose. By cultivating emotional awareness, you not only improve your mental and physical health but you also unlock the potential for meaningful transformation and fulfillment.

Identifying Emotional Triggers and Patterns

Emotional triggers are deeply personal stimuli that evoke intense emotional reactions, often without conscious awareness. They arise from past experiences, deeply held beliefs, or unresolved conflicts, acting as reminders of situations that once provoked similar feelings. Triggers can manifest through a range of sensations, from frustration to fear or sadness. These reactions are not random; they are shaped by the associations our minds create between present circumstances and past emotional events. They serve as a mirror reflecting unresolved issues, highlighting areas in need of attention and growth. Understanding these triggers provides a foundation for building emotional awareness and resilience.

Reactions to triggers often feel disproportionate to the immediate situation because they are rooted in deeper layers of experience. A critical comment, for instance, might provoke an intense reaction in someone who has unresolved insecurities or a history of criticism. The current event acts as a spark that reignites old emotional wounds, amplifying the response. Recognizing these triggers is not about assigning blame or invalidating emotions but about uncovering the source of the reaction. When identified, triggers can transform from sources of distress into tools for self-understanding and healing.

Journaling and self-reflection are invaluable practices for uncovering emotional patterns and identifying triggers. Writing provides a safe and structured outlet for processing thoughts and feelings, allowing individuals to observe recurring themes and reactions. By documenting specific situations that evoke strong emotional responses, patterns begin to emerge. These patterns reveal connections between past experiences and current emotions, shedding light on the underlying causes of triggers.

Self-reflection involves stepping back to evaluate emotional responses without judgment. It creates an opportunity to explore the "why" behind feelings and reactions. Questions such as "What about this situation make me feel upset?" or "Does this remind me of my past?" guide the process. Over time, these practices cultivate greater self-awareness, enabling individuals to recognize triggers more readily and respond with intention rather than impulsivity.

Practical exercises further support the identification and tracking of personal triggers. One effective approach is creating an emotional reaction log. This involves recording moments of heightened emotional response, including the event, thoughts, feelings, and physical sensations experienced at the time. By reviewing this log, patterns related to specific situations, people, or environments become apparent. This awareness is a crucial step in managing emotional triggers constructively.

Another exercise is the "five whys" technique, which involves asking "why" repeatedly to uncover the root cause of an emotional reaction. For example, if a comment made by a colleague or a friend feels upsetting, the first question might be, "Why did that comment bother me?" The response could be, "I feel undervalued by it." The next "why" could explore why that undervalued feeling is significant, leading to deeper insights about personal beliefs or previous experiences. This method helps peel back layers of emotional responses, exposing the core issues that fuel triggers.

Mindful observation is another valuable tool for recognizing triggers. By practicing mindfulness, you can learn to stay present and observe your emotions as they arise. This practice reduces the likelihood of being overwhelmed by feelings, creating a space to identify what has triggered the reaction. For instance, if frustration surfaces during a conversation, mindfulness allows for recognition of the emotion and its source without judgment. This awareness interrupts automatic reactions, fostering a more measured response.

Another helpful exercise involves body awareness. Physical sensations often accompany emotional triggers, such as tension in the chest, a racing heart, or clenched fists. Paying attention to these signals can provide early warnings of emotional activation. Acknowledging these sensations without resistance enhances the ability to identify triggers before they escalate into reactive behaviors.

Engaging in role-playing scenarios can also provide insights into triggers and emotional patterns. By imagining or reenacting challenging situations, individuals can explore their reactions in a controlled setting. This process allows for experimentation with alternative responses and the identification of underlying triggers in a non-confrontational way. It also builds confidence in handling similar situations in real life.

Recognizing and addressing triggers is not a one-time effort but an ongoing practice. As individuals grow and evolve, new triggers may emerge, reflecting deeper layers of personal experience or changing circumstances. By maintaining a commitment to self-awareness through practices like journaling, mindfulness, and self-reflection, the process becomes less daunting and more empowering. Each trigger identified becomes an opportunity for growth, reducing its power over time and fostering emotional stability.

Understanding emotional triggers and patterns is a transformative process that opens the door to greater emotional intelligence and well-being. By acknowledging the connections between past experiences and present reactions, you will gain insight into yourself and your needs. This understanding enhances relationships, decision-making, and overall quality of life. Emotional triggers are not obstacles but invitations to explore, understand, and heal, leading to a deeper sense of self-awareness and personal freedom.

Emotions play a vital role in shaping how individuals interact with their surroundings, make decisions, and build relationships. However, the way these emotions are expressed or processed determines whether they contribute positively or negatively to personal well-being and interpersonal connections. A healthy emotional response reflects self-awareness, control, and the ability to process feelings constructively. It aligns with the situation at hand, fostering understanding and resolution without causing harm to oneself or others. Healthy responses often involve the acknowledgment of emotions, clear communication, and actions that are thoughtful and deliberate.

In contrast, unhealthy emotional responses are characterized by reactions that may be disproportionate, impulsive, or destructive. They often stem from unprocessed feelings, unresolved past experiences, or deeply ingrained patterns. These reactions may manifest as excessive anger, withdrawal, or passive-aggressive behavior, among others. Unhealthy responses not only strain personal relationships but also lead to internal conflicts, impacting mental and physical health over time. Recognizing the distinction between these two forms of emotional expression is essential for developing emotional intelligence and fostering self-growth.

Factors such as upbringing, cultural norms, and personal trauma heavily influence emotional responses. Childhood experiences, for instance, play a significant role in shaping how individuals process and express emotions. A nurturing environment that encourages open dialogue about feelings often equips individuals with tools to respond healthily. Conversely, a background where emotions were dismissed or punished may lead to suppression, avoidance, or exaggerated expressions of feelings in adulthood. These early influences create templates for emotional regulation that can either empower or hinder individuals in managing their reactions effectively.

Cultural frameworks further shape emotional responses by dictating what is deemed acceptable or unacceptable. In some cultures, expressing emotions openly is encouraged as a sign of authenticity, while in others, restraint is valued as a marker of strength or decorum. These societal norms can either facilitate understanding and communication or suppress genuine emotional expression, leading to internal conflicts. The interplay between personal upbringing and cultural expectations often creates complex patterns that influence emotional responses across various contexts.

Trauma adds another layer of complexity, as it can profoundly alter how emotions are processed and expressed. Individuals who have experienced significant emotional or physical harm may develop heightened sensitivity to certain situations or struggle with managing their reactions. Trauma can lead to hyperarousal, where responses are overly intense, or to emotional numbing, where feelings are suppressed altogether. These patterns, while protective in the context of the original trauma, often persist in ways that hinder healthy emotional engagement. Understanding the impact of these experiences is crucial for breaking free from unhelpful patterns and fostering emotional resilience.

Transforming unhealthy emotional reactions into constructive behaviors requires intentional effort and the adoption of practical techniques. One effective approach is learning to pause before responding. This brief moment of reflection allows individuals to assess their feelings, consider the context, and choose a measured response rather than reacting impulsively. By practicing this pause regularly, it becomes easier to break cycles of automatic and often unproductive reactions.

Another valuable method is reframing negative thoughts associated with emotional triggers. For instance, rather than viewing a situation as a personal attack, individuals can reinterpret it as an opportunity for dialogue or understanding. This shift in perspective not only reduces emotional intensity but also fosters more constructive interactions. Over time, reframing helps to build resilience and adaptability, making it easier to handle challenging situations with composure.

Engaging in mindfulness practices enhances the ability to recognize and regulate emotions effectively. By focusing on the present moment without judgment, individuals develop a heightened awareness of their emotional states and the factors influencing them. This practice helps to create a sense of balance and control, reducing the likelihood of unhealthy responses. Regular mindfulness exercises, such as deep breathing or guided meditation, strengthen the connection between emotions and thoughtful actions.

Journaling provides another avenue for transforming unhealthy emotional patterns. Writing about experiences, triggers, and reactions offers an opportunity to reflect on recurring themes and identify areas for growth. This process encourages individuals to explore their feelings in a safe and structured way, uncovering insights that might otherwise remain hidden. Over time, journaling helps to clarify emotional needs and develop healthier ways of addressing them.

Therapeutic approaches, such as cognitive-behavioral strategies, can also aid in reshaping emotional responses. These methods focus on identifying and challenging unhelpful thought patterns that contribute to unhealthy reactions. By replacing these thoughts with more constructive beliefs, individuals can shift their emotional responses in a positive direction. Therapy also provides a supportive environment for addressing underlying issues, such as trauma or deeply ingrained beliefs, that fuel unhelpful emotional patterns.

Building a support system of trusted individuals is another key strategy for fostering healthier emotional responses. Sharing feelings with empathetic friends, family members, or mentors creates a sense of connection and validation, reducing the burden of processing emotions alone. This support network can also offer perspective, helping individuals to see situations more clearly and respond in ways that align with their values and goals.

Practicing emotional regulation techniques, such as grounding exercises, further enhances the ability to manage emotions constructively. Grounding involves redirecting attention to the present moment through sensory experiences, such as focusing on sounds, textures, or physical movements. These exercises help to reduce emotional overwhelm, creating space for thoughtful and deliberate responses. Regular practice of these techniques builds emotional stability, making it easier to handle challenging situations without resorting to unhealthy reactions.

Developing self-compassion is also integral to transforming emotional patterns. Recognizing that mistakes and setbacks are part of the human experience fosters a sense of understanding and kindness toward oneself. This attitude reduces self-criticism, which often exacerbates unhealthy emotional responses, and encourages a more balanced and constructive approach to personal growth.

Understanding and differentiating between healthy and unhealthy emotional responses is an ongoing process that requires self-awareness, reflection, and effort. By acknowledging the factors that shape emotional patterns and adopting practical techniques to address them, you can cultivate a greater sense of control and well-being. This journey not only enhances personal growth but also strengthens relationships and overall quality of life. Through intentional practice and support, the transformation from unhealthy reactions to constructive behaviors becomes an attainable and empowering reality.

Self-Reflective Questions

1. What emotions do I experience most frequently, and how do they influence my daily interactions and decisions?

2. When I feel overwhelmed or triggered, what patterns emerge in my thoughts, actions, or physical sensations?

3. How do I currently express my emotions, and do I feel that my expressions align with my true feelings?

4. Are there specific situations, people, or environments that consistently evoke strong emotional reactions in me? Why?

5. How have my upbringing or past experiences shaped my current relationship with emotions?

Transformative Exercises

1. Emotion Journaling:

Dedicate 10–15 minutes daily to writing about your emotional experiences. Note what emotions you felt, what triggered them, and how you responded. Over time, identify recurring patterns or themes in your emotional reactions.

2. Emotion Mapping:

Create a chart or diagram that links specific emotions to triggers, physical sensations, and habitual responses. This visual tool helps clarify how emotions manifest in your body and behavior, making them easier to understand and address.

3. **Pause and Label Practice**:
During moments of heightened emotion, take a moment to pause and mentally label the emotion you are experiencing (e.g., anger, sadness, or joy). This practice builds awareness and creates space for intentional responses.

4. **Mirror Exercise**:
Stand in front of a mirror and verbally describe how you are feeling, including any underlying causes or thoughts. Speaking aloud can help you process emotions and foster a deeper connection with your inner self.

5. **Emotion Check-In Routine**:
Set a timer for three specific times each day to check in with yourself. Ask: "What am I feeling right now? Why am I feeling this way? What do I need at this moment?" This routine helps you stay attuned to your emotions and needs throughout the day.

Chapter 3

Emotional Intelligence

{Managing Emotions Effectively}

Understanding Emotional Intelligence and Its Impact

Emotional intelligence, a critical aspect of personal growth and relational success, encompasses the ability to understand, manage, and utilize emotions in meaningful ways. It is a skill set that enhances communication, decision-making, and interpersonal interactions. The concept is rooted in self-awareness, self-regulation, and empathy, each contributing to a balanced and thoughtful approach to life's challenges. These components work together to help individuals not only understand their emotions but also respond to them constructively and effectively.

Self-awareness is the foundation of emotional intelligence. It involves recognizing and understanding one's emotional states and how they influence actions and decisions. A person with strong self-awareness can identify emotions without being overwhelmed or reactive. For instance, during a disagreement, recognizing feelings of frustration allows one to pause and assess the situation rather than reacting impulsively. This ability fosters clarity and provides an opportunity to choose a more constructive response.

Self-regulation builds upon self-awareness, emphasizing control and adaptability. It involves managing emotions in a way that aligns with one's values and goals. This does not mean suppressing feelings but rather channeling them in productive ways. For example, a leader facing a stressful situation may experience anxiety but chooses to remain calm, offering reassurance to their team instead of projecting tension. This form of regulation maintains stability and fosters trust, both in oneself and among others.

Empathy is the capability to understand and share in the feelings of others, this creates a room for deeper connections and improved communication. It goes beyond sympathy by enabling individuals to step into another person's perspective, fostering genuine understanding. Empathy plays a crucial role in building relationships, whether in personal settings or professional environments. For instance, a manager who notices a team member's discouragement might take time to listen, offer support, and adjust expectations, creating an environment of collaboration and mutual respect.

Emotional intelligence significantly influences success across various domains. In personal settings, it enhances relationships by promoting open communication, mutual respect, and conflict resolution. For instance, during a family disagreement, an emotionally intelligent individual might recognize rising tensions, calmly express their perspective, and encourage dialogue, ultimately leading to a more harmonious outcome. This approach prevents misunderstandings and strengthens bonds.

In professional environments, emotional intelligence is often a distinguishing factor among leaders and team members. It contributes to effective leadership, decision-making, and team dynamics. A manager with high emotional intelligence might handle a challenging situation, such as addressing poor performance, by balancing accountability with empathy. Instead of criticizing, they engage in a constructive conversation, offering guidance while understanding the underlying challenges. This approach not only addresses the issue but also motivates the individual and reinforces a positive work culture.

Scenarios further illustrate the impact of emotional intelligence in action. Consider a teacher working with a student struggling academically. Recognizing the student's frustration, the teacher acknowledges their feelings and offers encouragement, saying, "I see how hard you're trying, and I appreciate your effort.
Allow us to work together to figure this out" This empathetic response validates the student's emotions while fostering a supportive environment. The teacher's self-regulation prevents frustration from affecting the interaction, ensuring a calm and solution-focused approach.

In another example, a healthcare professional dealing with a distressed patient demonstrates emotional intelligence by remaining composed and empathetic. By actively listening and addressing concerns with compassion, they build trust and provide reassurance. This ability to manage personal emotions while understanding another's perspective ensures better patient outcomes and professional fulfillment.

Developing emotional intelligence requires consistent effort and intentional practice. One method is to reflect on emotional triggers and responses, identifying patterns that may hinder constructive interactions. Journaling or discussing these reflections with a trusted confidant can provide insights and foster growth. For example, recognizing a tendency to become defensive during criticism allows an individual to practice staying open-minded, focusing on the feedback rather than the perceived attack.

Mindfulness practices also enhance emotional intelligence by cultivating awareness and presence. Techniques such as deep breathing, meditation, or simply taking a moment to observe one's surroundings help regulate emotions and maintain focus. A mindful individual is better equipped to respond thoughtfully, even in challenging situations. For instance, during a heated discussion, pausing to take a deep breath can prevent escalation and allow for a more measured response.

Empathy can be developed by actively listening and seeking to understand others' perspectives without judgment. Engaging in conversations with curiosity and openness fosters connections and enhances understanding. For example, instead of dismissing a colleague's concerns during a project, taking the time to ask questions and acknowledge their feelings strengthens collaboration and trust.

Self-regulation can be improved by setting personal goals for emotional responses. For instance, committing to maintaining calm during stressful situations or practicing gratitude in moments of frustration helps build resilience. Over time, these intentional efforts create new habits, allowing individuals to approach challenges with greater composure and effectiveness.

In relationships, emotional intelligence promotes authenticity and meaningful connections. By recognizing and respecting one's emotions and those of others, interactions become more genuine and fulfilling. Whether in a romantic partnership, friendship, or professional relationship, the ability to understand and manage emotions fosters trust, mutual support, and shared growth.

The journey of cultivating emotional intelligence is one of ongoing self-discovery and improvement. It requires an openness to learning, a commitment to understanding emotions, and a willingness to adapt. Through consistent practice, individuals can enhance their ability to navigate life's complexities with grace and confidence. Emotional intelligence is not merely a skill but a way of approaching life that prioritizes understanding, connection, and purposeful action. It empowers individuals to handle challenges with resilience, build meaningful relationships, and achieve personal and professional success.

Techniques for Regulating Emotions in Challenging Situations

Maintaining emotional balance in difficult circumstances is an essential skill that strengthens resilience and fosters clarity. When faced with stress, understanding practical methods to regulate emotions can help prevent impulsive reactions and encourage thoughtful decision-making. Cultivating these techniques not only aids in reducing the intensity of immediate emotional responses but also supports long-term mental and emotional well-being.

Stressful situations often trigger physiological responses, such as increased heart rate, rapid breathing, and muscle tension. The first step toward regaining control is by recognizing these signs. Deep and focused breathing is one of the most effective tools to manage stress at the moment. A simple practice involves inhaling slowly through the nose, holding the breath briefly, and exhaling fully through the mouth. This process signals the nervous system to calm down, allowing a shift from a reactive to a composed state. Consistent practice of controlled breathing strengthens this response, making it easier to access during heightened stress.

Meditation is another powerful technique that enhances emotional regulation by fostering present-moment awareness. Sitting quietly, focusing on the breath or a calming word, and letting thoughts pass without judgment can reduce emotional intensity. Meditation trains the mind to respond with equanimity rather than reactivity, even during moments of discomfort. Over time, this practice rewires the brain to handle stress more effectively, promoting a steady and centered approach to life's challenges.

Visualization serves as a mental rehearsal, helping individuals prepare for or cope with triggering situations. By picturing a calm and composed reaction to a specific scenario, the mind creates a blueprint for actual behavior. For example, someone anticipating a difficult conversation might visualize speaking confidently and listening attentively, reinforcing a sense of readiness and control. Visualization combines mental focus with emotional intention, creating a sense of empowerment that reduces the perceived threat of the situation.

Responding mindfully to challenging circumstances involves a combination of self-awareness, intention, and deliberate action. One actionable step is to pause before responding. This pause, even if brief, creates space to assess the situation and choose a response aligned with one's values. For instance, if criticized, taking a moment to consider the validity of the feedback before reacting can shift the interaction from defensive to constructive.

Journaling provides a structured outlet to process emotions and explore potential responses. Writing down feelings and thoughts about a triggering event helps to externalize and analyze them, reducing their hold. Through reflection, patterns of emotional reactivity become clearer, and more thoughtful strategies for handling similar situations can be developed.

Journaling also serves as a reminder of growth and progress, reinforcing confidence in one's ability to manage emotions.

Physical movement can offer immediate relief from intense emotions. Activities such as walking, stretching, or engaging in a favorite form of exercise help release built-up tension and restore emotional balance. Movement redirects energy away from the stressor, allowing the mind to reset and approach the situation with renewed perspective. This practice also supports overall emotional health by reducing cortisol levels and increasing endorphins, contributing to a more stable mood.

Grounding techniques are invaluable for staying present during moments of emotional overwhelm. One effective method is the "five-four-three-two-one" exercise, which includes naming five things you can possibly see, four things to feel, three things you can listen to or hear, two things you can smell, and one thing you can easily taste or imagine. This practice shifts focus away from distressing thoughts and back to the physical world, creating a sense of safety and calm. Grounding can be adapted to different environments, making it a versatile tool for immediate emotional relief.

The role of self-compassion in emotional regulation cannot be overlooked. Treating oneself with kindness during challenging moments helps to reduce shame or frustration over emotional reactions. For example, instead of thinking, "I shouldn't feel this way," reframing the thought to "It's okay to feel this; I'm doing my best," fosters acceptance and encourages resilience. Self-compassion practices, such as writing supportive letters to oneself or engaging in soothing activities, strengthen emotional well-being and reinforce positive coping mechanisms.

Understanding triggers is essential for proactive emotional regulation. Triggers often stem from unresolved experiences, unmet expectations, or deeply held beliefs. Identifying these patterns requires reflection and honesty. Keeping a record of situations that provoke strong emotions, including thoughts and physical sensations, reveals recurring themes. Awareness of these triggers allows individuals to anticipate and prepare for them, reducing their impact over time.

For example, if public speaking triggers anxiety, preparation might include practicing the presentation multiple times, visualizing a calm delivery, and using deep breathing before taking the stage. Anticipating the trigger and employing strategies in advance reduces its emotional power, allowing for a more confident performance.

Setting intentions for how to handle challenging emotions can provide a clear framework for action. Creating personal mantras or affirmations, such as "I am calm and in control" or "I choose to respond with kindness," reinforces a mindset of resilience. Repeating these affirmations during stressful moments helps redirect focus and maintain composure. Over time, this practice strengthens emotional self-regulation and builds trust in one's ability to handle adversity.

Engaging in practices that build emotional resilience enhances overall regulation. Activities like gratitude journaling, spending time in nature, or fostering supportive relationships contribute to a foundation of emotional strength. These habits create a reserve of positivity that can be drawn upon during difficult times, making it easier to manage stress and maintain balance.

Emotional regulation is not about suppressing or avoiding emotions but rather learning to engage with them in ways that support growth and well-being. It requires patience, practice, and a willingness to experiment with different techniques. Each step taken toward emotional regulation contributes to greater self-awareness, stronger relationships, and a more empowered approach to life's challenges. By cultivating these skills, individuals create a foundation for navigating stress with confidence and grace, transforming challenges into opportunities for growth.

Enhancing Empathy and Building Emotional Connections

Empathy is a cornerstone of meaningful human interaction, allowing individuals to connect on a deeper level by understanding and sharing the feelings of others. It serves as the foundation for building trust and fostering genuine relationships, as it creates a sense of mutual respect and understanding. When someone feels truly heard and understood, barriers dissolve, and meaningful connections take root. Empathy is not merely about feeling for others but about being present in their experience, acknowledging their emotions, and validating their perspectives without judgment.

Trust and understanding emerge when empathy is practiced consistently, as it bridges emotional gaps and nurtures a sense of safety. People are drawn to those who demonstrate genuine concern and make an effort to see the world through their eyes. This effort fosters openness, reducing misunderstandings and encouraging honest communication. Empathy also plays a critical role in resolving conflicts, as it helps identify the underlying emotions driving disagreements. By addressing these emotions, individuals can work toward solutions that honor all perspectives.

Active listening is a powerful tool for enhancing emotional connections and demonstrating empathy. This practice goes beyond merely hearing words; it involves fully focusing on the speaker, observing nonverbal cues, and reflecting on their emotions. When people feel they have the undivided attention of another, they are more likely to share openly and honestly. Active listening requires setting aside assumptions and responding with thoughtful questions or affirmations, showing that the listener values the speaker's thoughts and feelings.

For example, if a friend expresses frustration about a challenging situation, responding with "It sounds like you're feeling overwhelmed. How can I support you?" not only acknowledges their emotions but also invites deeper conversation. This simple act of validation strengthens the bond between individuals and reinforces the importance of emotional connection. Active listening also helps clarify misunderstandings, as it ensures that both parties fully comprehend each other's viewpoints before responding.

Strengthening empathy in daily interactions can be achieved through deliberate practice and reflection. One effective exercise involves perspective-taking, which encourages individuals to imagine themselves in another person's situation. This practice cultivates an understanding of the emotions and challenges others may be experiencing, fostering greater compassion and patience. For instance, when encountering a colleague who appears irritable, instead of reacting defensively, one might consider the external pressures or personal struggles they might be facing.

Another powerful tool for building empathy is journaling with a focus on understanding others. Writing about interactions, reflecting on the emotions of those involved, and considering how different responses might have impacted the situation can deepen one's ability to relate to others. This habit not only sharpens emotional awareness but also promotes intentional behavior in future interactions.

Mindfulness practices can also enhance empathy by fostering presence and awareness in interactions. Taking a moment to pause, breathe, and center oneself before engaging with others allows for a more attentive and thoughtful response. Mindfulness reduces distractions and enhances the ability to tune into the emotions of others, creating a space for genuine connection.

Engaging in compassionate listening exercises is another way to strengthen empathy. This involves setting aside dedicated time to listen to someone without interrupting or offering solutions, focusing solely on understanding their perspective. By resisting the urge to provide immediate advice or share one's own experiences, the listener creates an environment where the speaker feels valued and supported. This practice builds trust and deepens emotional bonds.

Expressing gratitude is a simple yet impactful way to foster empathy and emotional connection. Acknowledging the contributions or positive qualities of others not only strengthens relationships but also encourages a culture of appreciation and mutual respect. Gratitude shifts focus from individual concerns to shared experiences, enhancing the ability to understand and connect with others on an emotional level.

Empathy also grows through exposure to diverse perspectives and experiences. Actively seeking out conversations with individuals from different backgrounds or viewpoints broadens understanding and challenges preconceived notions. This exposure fosters openness and adaptability, key components of empathy that enable individuals to relate to others more effectively.

Role-playing exercises can provide a hands-on approach to practicing empathy. In these activities, participants are asked to assume the perspective of someone else and respond to a scenario as that person would. This exercise helps individuals develop a deeper appreciation for the emotions and motivations of others, strengthening their capacity for empathetic responses in real-life situations.

The importance of empathy in personal and professional relationships cannot be overstated. It enhances communication, builds stronger connections, and fosters a sense of belonging. By practicing active listening, engaging in reflective exercises, and cultivating mindfulness, individuals can develop the skills necessary to deepen their emotional connections and create environments of trust and understanding. Empathy is a transformative practice that not only enriches relationships but also contributes to a more compassionate and harmonious world.

Self-Reflective Questions

1. How do I typically react to emotionally charged situations, and what patterns do I notice in my responses?

2. In what ways do my emotions impact the decisions I make, both positively and negatively?

3. How often do I take time to identify and label my emotions accurately before responding?

4. When faced with someone else's strong emotions, how do I approach understanding and addressing their feelings?

---

5. What are the areas of my emotional intelligence—self-awareness, self-regulation, empathy, motivation, or social skills—that I feel most and least confident in, and why?

Transformative Exercises

1. **Emotion Identification Journal**:
Spend five minutes daily recording the emotions you experience throughout the day. Note the situations that triggered these emotions, your immediate reactions, and how you handled them. Over time, analyze patterns and identify areas for improvement.

2. **Empathy Practice Roleplay**:

Go into partnership with a friend or your family member to practice active listening. Allow them to express a recent emotional experience while you focus on understanding their perspective without interrupting or offering solutions. Reflect on how this deepened your emotional connection.

3. **Pause and Reframe Exercise**:

When faced with an emotionally intense situation, pause for a moment. Take three deep breaths and ask yourself how you can view the situation from a different perspective. Practice responding in a calm and thoughtful way rather than reacting impulsively.

4. **Visualization for Self-Regulation**:

Visualize a challenging emotional moment in the past. Imagine how you would have handled it differently using calmness, clear communication, or empathy. Repeat this exercise with other scenarios to mentally rehearse improved responses.

5. **Emotional Check-In Alarm**:

Set an alarm three times a day as a reminder to pause and check in with yourself.

Ask, "What exactly do I feel right now, and why?" Write your observations and any other action(s) you can take to regulate and constructively channel those emotions.

Chapter 4

Healthy Relationships

{Building Meaningful Connections}

The Role of Trust and Vulnerability in Relationships

Vulnerability is the cornerstone of authentic relationships. It is the act of exposing one's inner self—thoughts, fears, dreams, and emotions—to another, fostering a deeper connection. Trust is born when two individuals allow themselves to be seen in their most unguarded moments. Without vulnerability, relationships can remain superficial, lacking the depth required for genuine intimacy.

When one person demonstrates vulnerability, it often encourages the other to do the same, creating a reciprocal dynamic where trust flourishes. Sharing experiences of failure, fear, or uncertainty can dismantle emotional walls and replace them with bridges of understanding. It is through such openness that bonds are solidified, as both individuals feel valued, heard, and understood.

Creating a safe environment for honest communication begins with cultivating a space free from judgment. When individuals know they can express themselves without fear of ridicule or dismissal, they are more likely to share openly. This involves active listening, where the listener offers undivided attention and avoids interjecting with unsolicited advice or criticism. A supportive listener not only acknowledges the speaker's words but also validates their feelings, showing genuine concern and interest.

Establishing boundaries is another critical component of fostering trust and vulnerability. Clear boundaries ensure that personal disclosures are respected and not misused. When individuals respect each other's limits, they signal that the relationship is a secure space where both parties can thrive emotionally.

Relationships often grow stronger when tested by challenges that require vulnerability. For instance, consider a couple facing financial hardship. One partner admits feeling overwhelmed and inadequate, fearing judgment for their inability to contribute equally. Instead of criticizing, the other responds with compassion, sharing their own fears and offering reassurance. This mutual openness transforms what could have been a divisive issue into an opportunity to strengthen their bond.

Another example can be found in friendships where vulnerability is embraced. Imagine a person struggling with anxiety confiding in a close friend. Instead of dismissing their concerns, the friend responds with understanding and shares their own experiences with mental health struggles. This exchange not only deepens their connection but also provides a foundation of mutual support.

The act of sharing personal stories can be transformative for relationships. Take, for example, a team leader who admits to their employees that they made a mistake on a project. Instead of trying to conceal the error, they openly address it, inviting input on how to rectify the situation. This display of vulnerability not only builds trust but also sets a tone of authenticity and collaboration within the team.

It is important to note that vulnerability does not mean oversharing or exposing oneself indiscriminately. It requires discernment to determine when and with whom to be vulnerable. Trust is a gradual process, built over time through consistent actions and mutual understanding. Taking small steps toward openness can help gauge the other person's receptiveness and ensure that the relationship is a safe space for vulnerability.

Strengthened through trust, relationships can withstand the trials of life with resilience. Vulnerability allows individuals to lean on one another during difficult times, creating a network of emotional support. It transforms relationships into sources of comfort and strength, enabling both parties to face challenges with a united front.

Fostering vulnerability within relationships also requires self-awareness. Understanding one's own emotions, fears, and desires is essential for articulating them to others. Self-reflection can uncover barriers to vulnerability, such as past traumas or fears of rejection. By addressing these barriers, individuals can approach their relationships with greater confidence and openness.

Relationships anchored in trust and vulnerability create ripple effects beyond the immediate connection. They model healthy emotional behavior for others, inspiring a culture of openness and understanding. In families, for example, parents who exhibit vulnerability with each other set an example for their children, teaching them the value of honesty and emotional transparency.

Vulnerability also plays a critical role in repairing fractured relationships. When trust has been compromised, the willingness to acknowledge mistakes and express regret can pave the way for reconciliation. Admitting fault and seeking forgiveness requires immense courage but can often reignite the connection between individuals.

In professional settings, vulnerability can enhance collaboration and teamwork. A leader who admits their own limitations or asks for help creates an environment where others feel empowered to do the same. This dynamic fosters innovation, as team members are more likely to share ideas and take risks when they feel supported.

While vulnerability is essential for building trust, it is equally important to recognize the potential risks involved. Not everyone will respond positively to openness, and some may misuse the information shared with them. It is vital to approach vulnerability with mindfulness, ensuring that trust is extended to those who have demonstrated reliability and respect.

Despite the risks, the rewards of vulnerability far outweigh its challenges. It is the foundation upon which meaningful connections are built, allowing individuals to experience relationships that enrich their lives. Trust and vulnerability are not static qualities but ongoing practices that require intention and effort. By prioritizing these practices, individuals can cultivate relationships that stand the test of time.

Whether in personal or professional relationships, vulnerability is the thread that binds individuals together. It transforms interactions from surface-level exchanges into profound connections rooted in trust and mutual respect. Through vulnerability, relationships become sanctuaries where authenticity thrives, fostering emotional well-being and resilience for all involved.

Effective Communication Skills for Emotional Clarity

Effective communication forms the backbone of meaningful relationships, acting as the bridge that connects individuals on a deeper emotional level. It is not merely about exchanging words but about ensuring that thoughts, emotions, and intentions are clearly conveyed and understood. The principles that govern effective communication are vital for fostering emotional clarity and nurturing healthy connections in all areas of life.

Active listening is a foundational element of effective communication. It requires focusing completely on the speaker, absorbing not only their words but also their tone and body language. This level of attentiveness ensures that the speaker feels valued and understood. It also minimizes misunderstandings, as the listener gains a clearer understanding of the speaker's message.

Clarity and brevity are equally crucial in communication. Expressing thoughts in a straightforward and concise manner avoids unnecessary confusion. When people communicate with purpose and precision, they reduce the likelihood of misinterpretation. It is also essential to be mindful of the timing and context in which conversations take place, as these factors can significantly impact the outcome.

Empathy is another critical principle. It involves understanding and sharing the feelings of another person, creating a sense of connection and support. Communicating with empathy allows individuals to validate each other's emotions and perspectives, fostering an environment of mutual respect.

The use of "I" statements is an invaluable tool in reducing conflicts and promoting emotional clarity. This communication approach shifts the focus from blaming others to expressing personal feelings and needs. For example, saying "I feel hurt when plans change unexpectedly" is more constructive than saying, "You always ruin our plans." The former invites dialogue and understanding, while the latter can provoke defensiveness and escalate tensions.

"I" statements empower individuals to take ownership of their emotions and experiences without assigning blame. They encourage open and honest conversations that prioritize resolution over conflict. This technique is particularly effective in addressing sensitive issues, as it reduces the likelihood of the other person feeling attacked or misunderstood.

To improve communication across various types of relationships, one must adapt their approach to suit the dynamics of each connection. In romantic relationships, for instance, expressing appreciation regularly can strengthen the bond between partners. Gratitude fosters a positive atmosphere, making it easier to address challenges when they arise.

In family settings, setting aside dedicated time for open conversations can help build stronger connections. Creating a routine where family members share their thoughts and feelings without interruptions encourages honest and respectful dialogue. It also allows individuals to address concerns before they escalate into larger issues.

Friendships thrive on honest and supportive communication. Taking the time to check in with friends and actively listen to their concerns demonstrates care and commitment. Avoiding assumptions and seeking clarification when needed ensures that misunderstandings do not erode the relationship.

Professional relationships require a balance of assertiveness and diplomacy. Being clear and respectful in expressing needs or expectations fosters collaboration and productivity. Providing constructive feedback, rather than criticism, helps maintain a positive working environment. Active listening in professional settings also promotes understanding and reduces the potential for miscommunication.

Nonverbal communication plays a significant role in effective interactions. Body language, facial expressions, and tone of voice can either reinforce or contradict the spoken message. Maintaining open body language, such as uncrossed arms and consistent eye contact, signals attentiveness and receptivity. A calm and steady tone conveys confidence and helps set the tone for productive conversations.

Asking open-ended questions is another strategy to enhance communication. Questions like "How does the situation make you feel?" or "Can you share your thoughts on this matter?" invite and let the other person share more than just a simple yes or no as his or her response. This approach demonstrates genuine interest and encourages a more in-depth exchange of ideas.

Reflecting on conversations and seeking feedback can also lead to continuous improvement in communication skills. Asking questions like "Did I explain that clearly?" or "How did my response make you feel?" allows for self-awareness and growth. It also reassures the other person that their perspective is valued.

Mindfulness in communication is about being fully present during interactions. This means setting aside distractions, such as electronic devices, and giving undivided attention to the conversation at hand. Mindful communication not only enhances understanding but also demonstrates respect and consideration for the other person.

Conflict resolution is an inevitable aspect of communication in relationships. Approaching disagreements with a calm and solution-focused mindset is crucial. Acknowledging the other person's perspective, even if it differs from one's own, shows respect and fosters collaboration. Compromises that address the needs of both parties strengthen the relationship rather than allowing conflicts to create distance.

Patience and persistence are necessary for mastering effective communication. Developing these skills is an ongoing process that requires effort and commitment. Practicing patience during challenging conversations allows emotions to settle, creating space for more constructive discussions. Persistence in applying communication techniques ensures that they become second nature over time.

Building effective communication skills is not only about addressing issues but also about creating opportunities for positive interactions. Sharing moments of joy, celebrating achievements, and expressing love and appreciation strengthen the emotional connection between individuals. Such interactions reinforce the foundation of the relationship, making it easier to weather difficult times.

Emotional clarity in communication enhances not only relationships but also personal well-being. When individuals express their emotions and needs effectively, they experience less frustration and greater satisfaction in their interactions. This clarity also reduces stress and promotes emotional resilience, enabling individuals to approach challenges with a balanced mindset.

Effective communication is a powerful tool that shapes the quality of our relationships and the emotional landscapes of our lives. By embracing its principles and consistently applying them, individuals can create meaningful connections that are grounded in trust, respect, and mutual understanding. The journey toward mastering communication is one of continuous learning and growth, offering endless opportunities to deepen bonds and enrich the human experience.

Balancing Independence and Togetherness

Healthy relationships thrive on a delicate balance between individuality and unity. Maintaining one's sense of self while being part of a partnership or friendship is not a contradiction but a fundamental element of emotional well-being and relational harmony. Losing oneself entirely in another person can lead to dependency and stifled growth, while too much independence can create emotional distance. The key lies in fostering a connection that honors personal identity while nurturing mutual respect and understanding.

Individuality serves as the foundation for authentic relationships. It encompasses personal values, passions, and aspirations, which shape one's unique perspective on life. When individuals maintain their distinct identity, they bring richness and depth to their relationships, ensuring they are built on genuine connection rather than a need for validation or approval. The act of retaining personal goals and interests not only cultivates self-respect but also sets the stage for a relationship in which both parties can flourish.

Supporting each other's growth is an essential aspect of fostering meaningful connections without crossing the boundary into over-dependence. Encouraging a partner or friend to pursue their ambitions, learn new skills, or explore interests independently demonstrates trust and confidence in their abilities. This support strengthens the bond between individuals, as it communicates a shared commitment to each other's well-being and success.

Over-dependence, on the other hand, can erode the foundation of a relationship. Relying excessively on one person for emotional stability or validation places undue pressure on the relationship and can lead to feelings of suffocation or resentment. Striking a balance involves recognizing that both individuals have unique needs, challenges, and strengths. It is about being there for one another without losing sight of personal responsibilities and boundaries.

Establishing a balance between independence and togetherness requires intentional effort. Open communication is a cornerstone of this process, as it allows individuals to express their needs and expectations honestly. Sharing thoughts about personal space, time apart, and shared activities ensures that both parties feel heard and respected. These conversations provide clarity and help avoid misunderstandings that could lead to conflict or dissatisfaction.

Trust is another critical component in achieving this balance. Trust allows individuals to feel secure in their relationship, even when they are apart. It removes the need for constant reassurance and fosters an environment where both parties can confidently pursue their personal goals. This sense of security enhances the quality of the time spent together, as it is free from underlying tensions or doubts.

Shared experiences are equally important in nurturing togetherness. Activities such as engaging in a hobby, volunteering, or setting goals together create opportunities for meaningful connection. These shared moments reinforce the bond while allowing room for individuality, as both parties contribute their unique perspectives and skills to the experience.

To help partners or friends strike a healthy balance, consider practical exercises that encourage reflection and intentional action. One such exercise involves creating a shared vision for the relationship. This can include discussing long-term goals, shared values, and mutual expectations. By aligning on these aspects, individuals can ensure that their independence and togetherness work in harmony.

Another exercise involves setting personal and shared boundaries. Each person identifies areas where they require personal space or time, as well as activities or commitments that they would like to share. This process not only helps in understanding each other's needs but also fosters respect for those boundaries, strengthening trust and communication.

Journaling can also be a valuable tool for individuals to reflect on their sense of independence and connection within the relationship. Writing about personal goals, emotions, and interactions can reveal patterns or areas that require adjustment. This self-awareness is crucial for maintaining balance and addressing any concerns constructively.

Engaging in regular check-ins is another effective exercise. Partners or friends can set aside time to discuss what is working well in their relationship and areas where they feel adjustments may be needed. These conversations should focus on solutions and mutual understanding rather than blame or criticism.

Mindful gratitude is an exercise that helps to reinforce appreciation for both individuality and shared experiences. Taking time to express gratitude for each other's unique qualities and contributions to the relationship nurtures a positive and supportive dynamic. This practice encourages individuals to value their differences while celebrating their unity.

Balancing independence and togetherness is not a static achievement but an ongoing process. Relationships evolve as individuals grow and circumstances change, requiring regular adjustments to maintain harmony. Flexibility and adaptability are key to ensuring that both parties feel fulfilled and connected.

This balance enriches relationships by creating an environment where both individuals can thrive. It reduces the risk of burnout or resentment, as neither person feels overburdened or overlooked. Instead, it fosters a partnership or friendship that is resilient, dynamic, and deeply rewarding.

Ultimately, the goal is to cultivate a relationship where individuality is cherished, and shared experiences are celebrated. By honoring personal identity while nurturing mutual respect and understanding, individuals can create meaningful connections that stand the test of time. This harmonious balance is not only a testament to the strength of the relationship but also a reflection of personal growth and emotional maturity.

Self-Reflective Questions

1. What qualities do I value most in my relationships, and how do I nurture those qualities?

2. How do I typically handle conflict or disagreements with others, and how does this impact my relationships?

3. In what ways do I balance my needs with the needs of others in my personal and professional connections?

4. How comfortable am I with being vulnerable in relationships, and what factors influence my willingness to share openly?

---

5. What steps do I take to ensure my relationships are based on trust, mutual respect, and healthy boundaries?

Transformative Exercises

1. Active Listening Practice:
Choose one interaction each day to practice active listening. Focus on fully understanding the other person's words, emotions, and perspective without interrupting or formulating your response prematurely. Reflect on how this enhances your connection.

2. Trust-Building Activity:
Identify one person in your life and commit to a trust-building action, such as following through on a promise or sharing a meaningful experience. Observe how this strengthens your bond.

3. **Daily Gratitude for Relationships**:
At the end of each day, write down three things you appreciate about the people in your life. Over time, share these thoughts with the individuals to foster positive connections.

4. **Role Reversal Exercise**:
During a disagreement, take a moment to imagine the situation from the other person's perspective. Write down what you think they might be feeling or needing, and use this insight to guide your approach to resolving the issue.

5. **Personal and Shared Goals Worksheet**:
With a partner or close friend, create a worksheet listing your individual goals and shared aspirations. Discuss how you can support each other's growth while maintaining your individuality and enhancing your connection.

Chapter 5

Self-Care

{Prioritizing Emotional Well-Being}

Designing a Personalized Self-Care Routine

A well-rounded self-care routine addresses emotional, physical, mental, and social aspects of an individual's well-being. Each component contributes to creating a harmonious life that aligns with personal values and needs. Emotional self-care often forms the core of this practice, as emotions directly influence thoughts, behaviors, and overall mental health. Integrating activities that nurture emotional resilience into a self-care routine is essential for long-term well-being.

Tailoring a routine to meet emotional needs requires self-awareness and a commitment to honoring individual preferences and limitations. Emotional needs can vary widely from person to person, influenced by factors such as personality, past experiences, and current circumstances. Reflecting on what brings comfort, balance, and a sense of grounding is key. For some, this might involve spending time in nature, while others may find journaling or creative expression more beneficial.

Designing a personalized self-care plan begins with a thorough assessment of current habits and emotional states. Start by identifying areas of life that feel out of balance or neglected. For instance, if stress is a recurring issue, relaxation techniques might take priority. If feelings of disconnection are present, incorporating activities that foster meaningful interactions could be vital.

Once needs are identified, prioritize them based on their impact on emotional well-being. Break these needs into actionable components to ensure the routine feels manageable rather than overwhelming. Begin by establishing a list of activities that align with these priorities. For example, deep breathing exercises, short walks, or moments of mindfulness may be included for stress reduction, while time spent with loved ones or participating in a hobby could address social and creative needs.

Structuring the routine requires thoughtful planning. A step-by-step approach can help ensure it becomes a consistent practice rather than a fleeting effort. Start with small, achievable goals that fit seamlessly into daily or weekly schedules. For instance, set aside five minutes each morning for intentional breathing or gratitude reflection. Gradually build on these initial practices by introducing additional activities as they become second nature.

Accountability can enhance adherence to the self-care routine. Sharing goals with a trusted friend or family member can create a sense of mutual encouragement. Alternatively, keeping a journal to track progress and reflect on emotional shifts can provide insight into the effectiveness of the routine. Adjustments should be made as needed to accommodate changing circumstances or preferences.

Flexibility is crucial in maintaining a personalized self-care routine. Life often presents unexpected challenges, and rigid adherence to a routine may not always be possible. Viewing self-care as an adaptable practice rather than a fixed schedule allows for resilience and creativity in finding ways to nurture emotional health even during busy or difficult times.

A balanced self-care routine extends beyond individual activities to include boundaries that protect emotional energy. Saying no to commitments that feel draining or prioritizing time for rest can be as significant as the self-care activities themselves. Boundaries serve as a foundation for preserving the emotional space needed to recharge and refocus.

Incorporating self-reflection into the routine can help deepen its impact. Taking a few moments at the end of each day or week to assess how certain practices influenced emotional well-being can provide valuable feedback. This reflection can highlight which activities are most effective and which might need adjustment or replacement.

Community involvement can also play a role in self-care. Engaging in group activities, whether through volunteering, exercise classes, or support groups, offers opportunities for connection and shared experiences. These interactions can foster a sense of belonging and provide an emotional boost that complements individual self-care efforts.

Simplicity often ensures sustainability. Overloading a routine with numerous activities can feel burdensome and counterproductive. Choosing a few core practices that resonate deeply and incorporating them consistently is often more impactful than attempting to do too much. The goal is not to create another source of stress but to cultivate moments of peace and self-nourishment.

Celebrating progress and acknowledging the benefits of self-care reinforces its importance. Small wins, such as feeling more centered after a meditation session or experiencing better focus after a good night's sleep, serve as reminders of the value of prioritizing emotional well-being. Recognizing these positive outcomes can motivate continued commitment to the routine.

Ultimately, designing a self-care routine is a deeply personal process that evolves with time. It reflects a commitment to honoring one's emotional needs and fostering resilience in the face of life's challenges. By dedicating time and energy to this practice, individuals create a foundation for personal growth, healing, and true emotional freedom.

Stress Management Techniques for Everyday Life

Stress often stems from a variety of sources, each leaving its imprint on emotional and physical well-being. Workplace demands, financial pressures, relationship challenges, and health concerns frequently top the list. Everyday irritants like heavy traffic, long queues, or unexpected disruptions can also contribute to stress, compounding its impact over time. When unaddressed, prolonged stress may result in irritability, fatigue, anxiety, or even physical symptoms such as headaches and weakened immunity. Understanding these sources and their effects lays the groundwork for effective management techniques that prioritize emotional stability and personal well-being.

Managing stress begins with identifying triggers and observing how they influence mood and behavior. Awareness serves as a compass, guiding individuals toward strategies that mitigate these effects and promote resilience. Time management is a practical tool that reduces overwhelm by organizing responsibilities into manageable portions. Prioritizing tasks, delegating when appropriate, and allowing for flexibility are key elements in this approach. By breaking larger goals into smaller steps, individuals can experience a sense of accomplishment that reduces feelings of being overwhelmed.

Relaxation techniques play a vital role in stress relief by counteracting the body's physiological response to tension. Deep breathing exercises are particularly effective in calming the nervous system. In moments of heightened stress, taking slow, intentional breaths helps lower heart rate and encourage relaxation. Progressive muscle relaxation, which involves tensing and releasing muscle groups sequentially, can also release physical tension and restore a sense of calm.

Creative outlets provide another avenue for alleviating stress by offering an opportunity for self-expression and mental reprieve. Activities such as painting, writing, gardening, or playing an instrument allow individuals to channel their emotions productively, creating a sense of accomplishment and joy. Even those without prior experience in creative endeavors can benefit from the process, as the act of focusing on an enjoyable task naturally shifts attention away from stressors.

Quick strategies for managing stress during busy moments are essential for maintaining composure in fast-paced environments. Mindful pauses, where individuals momentarily shift their focus to the present moment, can provide immediate relief. For instance, taking 30 seconds to concentrate on the sensation of the breath or observing surroundings without judgment can create a mental reset. Similarly, grounding exercises, such as identifying five things seen, four things heard, three things touched, two things smelled, and one thing tasted, can anchor awareness and reduce feelings of overwhelm.

Physical movement serves as a natural stress reliever, as it helps release endorphins and improve mood. Even brief stretches or a short walk can disrupt stress patterns and invigorate the mind. Incorporating physical activity into daily routines, such as walking during lunch breaks or opting for stairs over elevators, ensures consistent benefits without requiring significant time commitments.

Maintaining boundaries is another critical aspect of stress management. Overcommitment often leads to burnout, as individuals struggle to meet the demands placed upon them. Saying no to unnecessary obligations or setting limits on work hours creates space for rest and rejuvenation. Boundaries also extend to digital distractions, such as constant notifications or excessive screen time, which can compound stress. Designating specific times to disconnect from devices fosters mental clarity and promotes relaxation.

Connecting with others provides emotional support and perspective during stressful times. Sharing concerns with trusted friends, family members, or support groups can reduce feelings of isolation and provide valuable insights. Additionally, humor and lighthearted conversations often serve as effective stress relievers, offering a much-needed break from seriousness.

Sleep plays an integral role in stress management by allowing the body and mind to recover. Poor sleep exacerbates stress by impairing cognitive function and emotional regulation. Establishing a consistent bedtime routine that includes calming activities, such as reading or taking a warm bath, signals the body to prepare for rest. Limiting caffeine intake and avoiding screens before bed further enhances sleep quality.

Diet also influences stress levels, as nutrient-rich foods provide the energy needed to cope with daily challenges. Consuming balanced meals that include fruits, vegetables, whole grains, and lean proteins supports physical and mental health. Conversely, excessive consumption of sugar, caffeine, or processed foods can contribute to irritability and fatigue, making stress more difficult to manage. Staying hydrated throughout the day is equally important, as dehydration can mimic or exacerbate stress-related symptoms.

Adopting a gratitude practice can shift focus away from stressors and toward positive aspects of life. Writing down three things to be grateful for each day cultivates a mindset of appreciation, reducing the emotional burden of challenges. This practice encourages reflection on moments of joy or success, even amidst adversity, fostering a balanced perspective.

Engaging in activities that bring joy or relaxation can counteract stress by activating the body's relaxation response. Whether through listening to music, spending time in nature, or enjoying a favorite hobby, these moments of pleasure serve as reminders of the importance of self-care. Scheduling regular "me time" ensures that such activities are prioritized rather than treated as afterthoughts.

Professional support may be beneficial when stress becomes unmanageable. Therapists, counselors, or coaches can provide guidance tailored to individual needs, equipping individuals with coping strategies that align with their circumstances.

Seeking help is a proactive step that demonstrates self-awareness and a commitment to well-being.

Stress management is not a one-size-fits-all solution but rather a personalized process that evolves with time and circumstances. By incorporating practical tools, quick relief strategies, and consistent habits, individuals can create a foundation for enduring resilience. Recognizing the impact of stress and addressing it proactively empowers individuals to maintain emotional balance and approach life's challenges with clarity and confidence.

The Connection Between Physical and Emotional Health

Physical health and emotional well-being are intricately connected, each exerting profound influence over the other. The mind and body operate as an interconnected system, meaning that disruptions in one domain inevitably affect the other. When the body is well-nourished, active, and rested, emotional balance becomes easier to sustain. Conversely, emotional strain can manifest in physical symptoms, further underscoring this connection. Recognizing and honoring this relationship is essential for cultivating a holistic approach to self-care.

The quality of nutrition has a direct impact on emotional states, as the nutrients consumed fuel both physical energy and brain function. A diet rich in whole foods such as fruits, vegetables, whole grains, lean proteins, and healthy fats supports the production of neurotransmitters that regulate mood. For instance, omega-3 fatty acids, found in foods like salmon and flaxseed, are associated with improved emotional stability. Conversely, excessive consumption of processed foods, sugars, and unhealthy fats can contribute to mood swings and fatigue, amplifying feelings of stress or sadness.

Exercise is another critical factor in this interplay, as physical activity promotes the release of endorphins, which are natural mood enhancers. Regular movement reduces stress hormones like cortisol while increasing serotonin levels, fostering feelings of calm and contentment. Beyond its immediate benefits, consistent exercise improves overall resilience by enhancing sleep quality, boosting self-esteem, and promoting mental clarity. Activities need not be strenuous to be effective—gentle practices such as walking, stretching, or yoga can also yield significant emotional benefits.

Sleep serves as a foundation for both physical restoration and emotional regulation. During sleep, the body repairs tissues, consolidates memories, and processes emotions. Insufficient rest impairs cognitive function, exacerbates irritability, and weakens the immune system, creating a cycle where poor sleep worsens emotional health and vice versa. Establishing a consistent sleep schedule and creating a calming bedtime routine can greatly enhance both physical and emotional resilience.

The reciprocal relationship between physical and emotional health becomes especially evident when considering the impact of stress. Chronic stress can suppress the immune system, increase the risk of cardiovascular issues, and lead to chronic pain conditions. On the emotional side, prolonged stress fosters feelings of anxiety, restlessness, or burnout. Implementing stress-reducing practices such as mindfulness, breathing exercises, or progressive muscle relaxation mitigates these effects, benefiting both mind and body.

Emotional well-being similarly influences physical health, often in subtle but profound ways. Positive emotions, such as gratitude, joy, and hope, have been shown to lower blood pressure, improve immune function, and reduce inflammation.

Conversely, unresolved emotional distress may manifest physically through headaches, digestive issues, or fatigue. These symptoms often serve as reminders to address underlying emotional needs, rather than dismissing them as unrelated ailments.

Case studies offer compelling evidence of how lifestyle changes can transform emotional well-being. For instance, consider an individual who struggled with persistent anxiety and low energy. Through incremental changes—replacing sugary snacks with balanced meals, incorporating 30 minutes of daily movement, and establishing a relaxing bedtime ritual—they reported significant improvements in both mood and vitality. These adjustments created a positive feedback loop where improved physical health bolstered emotional resilience, enabling them to cope more effectively with challenges.

Another example involves a professional dealing with high-pressure work environments and disrupted sleep patterns. By prioritizing restorative habits such as mindful eating, short afternoon walks, and consistent wind-down periods before bed, they found themselves less reactive to stress and more capable of maintaining focus. These changes not only reduced physical symptoms like tension headaches but also enhanced their overall sense of well-being.

Cultivating balance between physical and emotional health requires consistent effort and personalized strategies. While general guidelines—such as consuming nutrient-rich foods, engaging in regular movement, and honoring the need for rest—apply broadly, individual preferences and needs should guide the specifics. For instance, some may find joy in group fitness classes, while others prefer solitary hikes or creative dance routines. Similarly, nutritional choices should align with taste preferences, cultural traditions, and any dietary restrictions, ensuring that healthy eating feels sustainable rather than restrictive.

It's also worth acknowledging the role of social support in bridging the physical-emotional connection. Sharing meals with loved ones, participating in group activities, or simply connecting with supportive individuals fosters emotional nourishment alongside physical care. These interactions remind individuals that health is not solely an individual endeavor but a communal experience, enriched by relationships and shared goals.

Ultimately, understanding the interplay between physical health and emotional well-being empowers individuals to make informed choices that enhance their quality of life. By addressing both domains holistically, individuals can foster a sense of harmony that sustains them through life's challenges and opportunities alike.

Self-Reflective Questions

1. What activities or habits currently bring me the most joy and relaxation, and how can I prioritize them in my daily routine?

2. How well do I listen to my body's signals for rest, nourishment, or movement, and what changes might I make to honor these needs?

3. In what ways do I neglect my emotional or physical health, and what underlying beliefs or habits contribute to this neglect?

4. How do I currently manage stress, and are my strategies helping or hindering my overall well-being?

5. What boundaries do I need to set or enforce to protect my time, energy, and emotional health?

Transformative Exercises

1. **Personal Self-Care Assessment:**
Create a list of your daily activities and rate how each impacts your emotional and physical well-being. Identify one or two changes to improve balance and reduce stress.

2. **Mindful Morning Ritual:**
Dedicate the first 10–15 minutes of your day to an activity that

centers you, such as meditation, journaling, or light stretching. Reflect weekly on how this impacts your emotional state.

3. **Self-Care Planner**:

Design a weekly schedule that incorporates at least one self-care activity per day. Include activities for physical, emotional, and mental health, and review your progress at the end of the week.

4. **Gratitude Journaling**:

Write down three things you are grateful for each evening, focusing on aspects of your life that enhance your well-being. Reflect on how practicing gratitude influences your perspective.

5. **Stress Relief Toolkit**:

Create a personalized toolkit with items or activities that help you manage stress (e.g., calming music, aromatherapy, a favorite book, or a breathing exercise).
Use it whenever you feel overwhelmed and note its effectiveness.

Chapter 6

Boundary Setting

{Protecting Your Emotional Space}

Understanding the Importance of Healthy Boundaries

Emotional boundaries are the limits we set to protect our mental and emotional well-being from external pressures and encroachments. They define where one person's emotional state ends and another's begins, ensuring clarity and mutual respect in interactions. These boundaries serve as safeguards, allowing individuals to maintain their sense of identity, prioritize their emotional needs, and foster balanced relationships. Without them, people often find themselves overwhelmed, overextended, or misunderstood, which can lead to stress, resentment, and emotional burnout. Establishing clear limits is not an act of isolation but rather a way to enhance connections by creating an environment of mutual understanding and respect.

Identifying where boundaries are needed begins with self-awareness. Reflecting on moments that leave you feeling drained, resentful, or violated often reveals areas where boundaries are lacking. For instance, consistently saying yes to requests at the expense of your well-being or enduring conversations that leave you emotionally depleted might signal a need for firmer limits. It's also helpful to observe patterns in relationships, such as recurring conflicts or feelings of being taken for granted, as these often indicate a boundary issue. Emotional and physical cues like stress, anxiety, or exhaustion are invaluable in highlighting situations or interactions that require boundaries. Once identified, it becomes easier to address these areas and create a healthier balance.

A structured approach to setting boundaries can make the process more manageable and effective. Begin by clearly defining what you need and why it matters. For example, you might need uninterrupted time after work to decompress or request that personal topics remain off-limits in professional settings. Once your needs are clear, communicate them assertively but respectfully. Use "I" statements to express your perspective without assigning blame, such as, "I need some quiet time after work to recharge; I hope you can support me in this." Consistency is key in reinforcing these boundaries. If someone crosses a line, gently remind them of the agreed-upon limits. Flexibility may be required, but it should not come at the expense of your emotional well-being. Establishing and maintaining boundaries requires patience and practice, but it ultimately strengthens relationships and fosters mutual respect.

Boundaries in professional environments are equally critical. They prevent overextension and promote productivity by ensuring roles and expectations are clear. Start by identifying tasks or behaviors that hinder your ability to perform effectively, such as excessive after-hours communication or unclear responsibilities. Address these issues openly with colleagues or supervisors, focusing on solutions rather than blame. For instance, you might say, "I've noticed responding to work emails late at night affects my focus the next day. I'd like to set a boundary to manage my time better." Respectfully standing firm on your limits reinforces their importance and encourages others to honor them. Strong boundaries at work contribute to a healthier dynamic where mutual respect and accountability thrive.

Relationships flourish when boundaries are respected, as they create an atmosphere of trust and understanding. Setting limits in personal interactions involves recognizing your emotional triggers and communicating them honestly. For instance, if a friend frequently makes jokes at your expense, calmly expressing how this affects you can prevent future discomfort. It is equally important to respect the boundaries of others, listening and adapting as necessary. Boundaries are not meant to be rigid walls but flexible parameters that evolve with the relationship. They empower individuals to be authentic while fostering connections built on mutual care and consideration.

In summary, emotional boundaries are essential for maintaining personal well-being and cultivating healthy relationships. By identifying areas in life where boundaries are needed and employing a clear framework for setting and reinforcing them, individuals can protect their emotional space while enhancing their connections with others. The practice of boundary setting is a lifelong skill that promotes self-respect and fosters harmonious interactions across personal and professional domains.

Recognizing and Responding to Boundary Violations

Boundary violations can manifest in various ways, often leaving individuals feeling uneasy, disrespected, or overwhelmed. Recognizing these signs is essential for maintaining emotional balance and fostering healthy interactions. Emotional cues such as frustration, resentment, or a sense of being taken advantage of are often indicators that a limit has been crossed. Physical symptoms like tension, fatigue, or an inability to focus might also arise when boundaries are repeatedly ignored. Behavioral patterns such as avoiding certain individuals or situations can further highlight underlying issues. Acknowledging these signs is the first step in addressing and preventing ongoing violations.

Asserting oneself in the face of boundary violations can feel intimidating, especially for those who prioritize harmony or fear confrontation. However, standing firm does not necessitate aggression or hostility. Approaching such situations with calmness and clarity can create an environment for productive dialogue. It is important to communicate your feelings and needs without placing blame, using language that emphasizes personal experiences. For example, phrases like "I feel uncomfortable when…" or "I need some time to myself…" can convey your perspective while maintaining respect for the other party. Practicing this form of expression helps diminish guilt or fear by focusing on your rights to emotional well-being rather than framing the discussion as a conflict.

Responding constructively to boundary violations involves maintaining composure and seeking resolution rather than escalation. If someone continually interrupts your work despite prior requests for space, you might gently remind them, "I understand this is important to you, but I need this time to focus. Let's discuss it later." If a friend disregards your preferences in conversations, you could say, "I value our discussions, but I feel uneasy when certain topics are brought up. Let's focus on things we both enjoy." These approaches prioritize mutual understanding while reinforcing your limits.

In situations where repeated violations occur, more assertive measures may be required. This might involve restating your boundary firmly or seeking support from a third party if necessary. For example, in a professional setting, documenting instances where your boundaries were crossed and addressing them with a supervisor can establish accountability. In personal relationships, expressing the impact of repeated violations on your connection can help the other person understand the seriousness of the issue. Constructive handling of such situations underscores your commitment to emotional well-being and the health of your relationships.

Consistency is critical when addressing boundary violations. Allowing occasional breaches can send mixed signals, making it harder for others to respect your limits. By standing firm and reiterating your expectations, you establish the importance of your boundaries and encourage others to uphold them. This consistency also reinforces your own confidence in setting and maintaining limits, reducing the likelihood of guilt or self-doubt.

Repairing relationships after a boundary violation requires mutual effort and understanding. Acknowledging the breach and discussing how to prevent future occurrences can strengthen the bond between individuals. For instance, if a family member oversteps by sharing private information, an open conversation about the importance of confidentiality can rebuild trust. By addressing violations constructively, you can transform them into opportunities for growth and deeper connection.

The process of recognizing and responding to boundary violations is integral to protecting emotional space and fostering respectful interactions. Awareness of the signs that a boundary has been crossed, combined with the ability to assert oneself confidently, lays the foundation for healthier relationships. Constructive responses ensure that limits are respected without damaging connections, emphasizing the importance of mutual understanding and care. Through consistent practice, individuals can safeguard their well-being while cultivating environments where boundaries are honored and valued.

Assertive Communication for Maintaining Boundaries

Assertive communication is a method of expressing thoughts, feelings, and needs clearly and respectfully. Unlike passive communication, which often involves ignoring personal needs to avoid conflict, assertive communication ensures that personal boundaries are upheld without compromising respect for others. On the other hand, it avoids the hostility or domineering tone associated with aggressive communication, which prioritizes one's needs at the expense of others. Assertive communication creates a balanced interaction where honesty and respect coexist, fostering mutual understanding and reinforcing personal boundaries.

Expressing needs assertively involves recognizing the validity of your feelings and communicating them in a way that does not diminish the feelings of others. It starts with self-awareness—understanding your own emotions, needs, and the reasons behind them. From this understanding, you can frame your requests in a manner that is clear, direct, and free of judgment or blame. For example, instead of saying, "You never listen to me," an assertive approach might be, "I feel unheard when I'm interrupted. I'd appreciate it if we could wait for each other to finish speaking."

Respecting others while asserting your needs involves a balance of honesty and empathy. Empathy ensures that while advocating for your needs, you also acknowledge the perspective and feelings of the other person. This balance creates an atmosphere where your boundaries are more likely to be respected without causing defensiveness or conflict. For instance, saying, "I understand you have a lot on your plate, but I need some uninterrupted time to focus," acknowledges the other person's situation while reinforcing your need for space.

Templates or scripts can be helpful for navigating conversations about boundaries, especially in situations where emotions might run high or the stakes are significant. For instance, when addressing someone who frequently interrupts your personal time, you could say, "I value our relationship, but I need some quiet time each evening to recharge. Let's schedule a time that works for both of us to talk." In a professional context, if a colleague repeatedly assigns tasks outside your role, you might assert, "I appreciate your trust in my abilities, but I need to focus on my current responsibilities. Could we discuss alternative solutions?"

Assertive communication requires consistency to maintain boundaries effectively. Mixed signals or wavering on established limits can undermine their importance. Reinforcing boundaries with clear, respectful communication ensures that others understand their significance. For instance, if someone continues to disregard your boundary after an initial conversation, reiterating your stance calmly yet firmly, such as, "I've mentioned before that this time is important for my work. Let's find another way to address this issue," reinforces your commitment to maintaining your emotional space.

Building confidence in assertive communication can involve practice and preparation. Role-playing scenarios with a trusted friend or mentor can help refine your tone and wording, ensuring that you come across as firm but not confrontational. Visualizing the conversation beforehand and rehearsing key points can reduce anxiety, allowing you to approach the situation with clarity and calmness. Practicing assertiveness in low-stakes situations can also build the skills and confidence needed for more challenging conversations.

Incorporating "I" statements into assertive communication is an effective technique to express your needs without assigning blame. These statements focus on your feelings and needs, making it easier for the other person to understand your perspective without feeling attacked. For example, saying, "I feel overwhelmed when tasks are added to my workload without notice. I'd appreciate it if we could discuss deadlines in advance," shifts the focus to your experience rather than placing blame on the other party.

Assertive communication also involves active listening. Truly hearing the other person's concerns or perspective demonstrates that you value their input, even while maintaining your boundaries. Reflecting back what you've heard, such as, "It sounds like you're feeling stressed about meeting the deadline. I'd still need to prioritize my current projects, but let's explore how I can support you," shows understanding while standing firm on your limits.

It is important to recognize that not everyone will respond positively to boundary-setting, especially if they have previously benefited from a lack of boundaries. In such cases, maintaining a calm and composed demeanor is key. Repeating your boundary, if necessary, can reinforce its importance without escalating the situation. For example, if someone reacts negatively to your request for space, calmly reiterating, "I hear your concerns, but I still need this time to focus on myself," underscores your commitment to protecting your emotional well-being.

Assertive communication is not about winning or dominating an interaction. It is about mutual respect and the recognition that healthy relationships require honesty, understanding, and boundaries. Over time, consistently practicing assertive communication can improve relationships, build self-esteem, and establish an environment where emotional needs are met and respected. Through clear, respectful dialogue, individuals can protect their emotional space while fostering stronger, more balanced connections with others.

Self-Reflective Questions

What specific situations or interactions leave me feeling emotionally drained, and how do they impact my overall well-being?

Are there areas in my life where I feel resentful or taken advantage of, and what role do unclear boundaries play in these feelings?

How do I typically respond when someone crosses a line, and does my reaction effectively protect my emotional needs?

What fears or beliefs hold me back from setting firmer boundaries, and how might they stem from past experiences or learned behaviors?

How do I differentiate between being assertive and being confrontational, and what can I do to feel more confident in expressing my limits?

Transformative Exercises

1. Boundary Inventory Journal:

Reflect on your daily interactions over the course of a week. Identify moments where you felt your emotional or physical boundaries were compromised. Write down what you felt, what you wished you had communicated, and what you would do differently next time.

2. **Role-Playing Scenarios**:

Practice boundary-setting conversations with a trusted friend or mentor. Create scenarios based on real-life experiences, such as handling a demanding coworker or declining a personal favor, and refine your approach through feedback.

3. **Boundary Mapping Exercise**:

Draw a circle representing your emotional space. Within the circle, write down the behaviors, interactions, and activities you find acceptable. Outside the circle, list the actions or situations you no longer want to tolerate. Use this as a visual reminder of your limits.

4. **Assertiveness Practice with "I" Statements**:

Write down five boundary-setting phrases using "I" statements tailored to your current challenges. For instance, "I need uninterrupted time to focus on my work in the mornings. Let's discuss it after lunch." Practice saying these phrases aloud until they feel natural.

5. **Reflection Through Visualization**:

Close your eyes and imagine a boundary you want to establish. Picture yourself confidently expressing it and receiving a positive response. Consider how it feels to protect your emotional space and carry that clarity into your real-life interactions.

Chapter 7

Mindfulness And Resilience

{Staying Grounded And Strong}

The Practice of Mindfulness for Emotional Stability

Mindfulness is the deliberate practice of focusing one's attention on the present moment while observing thoughts, emotions, and sensations without judgment. It cultivates a sense of awareness that anchors the mind, offering clarity amidst life's complexities. By engaging with the present, mindfulness fosters emotional stability, allowing individuals to manage reactions effectively rather than being overwhelmed by them. This intentional focus nurtures a greater sense of control, reducing the emotional turbulence often triggered by stress, anxiety, or unresolved internal conflicts. Through mindfulness, one develops a profound connection to their inner world, encouraging thoughtful responses over impulsive reactions.

One of the key contributions of mindfulness to emotional balance lies in its capacity to create space between stimulus and response. Instead of reacting impulsively to a challenging situation, mindfulness provides a pause to assess emotions and choose a constructive course of action. This practice enhances emotional resilience, helping individuals remain composed even in the face of adversity. Furthermore, mindfulness helps identify recurring emotional patterns, empowering individuals to understand and address the root causes of their reactions. This awareness enables healthier emotional regulation and fosters personal growth.

Daily mindfulness exercises offer practical tools to strengthen emotional stability. A simple yet powerful exercise is conscious breathing, where attention is placed on each inhalation and exhalation. Focusing on the breath anchors the mind and calms the nervous system, making it a valuable tool during moments of heightened stress or agitation. For example, practicing deep breathing for five minutes during a stressful workday can provide immediate relief, promoting a sense of grounding and emotional clarity.

Another effective exercise is the body scan, which involves paying attention to physical sensations from head to toe. By slowly directing awareness to each part of the body, one can release tension and cultivate a deeper connection to the present moment. This practice is particularly helpful for managing anxiety or restlessness, as it redirects focus away from racing thoughts and back to the physical experience. Over time, this exercise also strengthens the mind-body connection, promoting holistic well-being.

Mindful observation of thoughts and emotions further enhances emotional stability. By sitting quietly and observing one's inner dialogue without attachment or judgment, it becomes easier to recognize habitual patterns that may lead to stress or negative self-perception. This practice fosters self-compassion, encouraging a kinder and more accepting attitude toward oneself. For example, rather than criticizing oneself for feeling angry, mindfulness allows the emotion to be acknowledged without judgment, paving the way for understanding and resolution.

Mindfulness also sharpens self-awareness, a cornerstone of emotional intelligence. By observing thoughts and feelings as they arise, individuals can identify triggers, unmet needs, and personal values more clearly. This heightened awareness contributes to better decision-making, as choices are made with greater alignment to one's true priorities. For instance, mindfulness can help someone recognize that their frustration stems not from an external event but from an internal expectation, allowing them to address the situation with clarity and compassion.

The impact of mindfulness extends beyond individual practice, influencing interpersonal relationships as well. By cultivating present-moment awareness, individuals become more attuned to the emotions and needs of others, fostering deeper connections and understanding. Active listening, a mindful approach to communication, enables individuals to engage fully in conversations without distractions or preconceived judgments. This practice not only strengthens relationships but also reduces misunderstandings and conflicts.

Mindfulness can be seamlessly integrated into daily routines through intentional moments of presence. For example, while drinking a cup of tea, one can focus entirely on the taste, warmth, and aroma of the beverage. This practice transforms an ordinary activity into an opportunity for mindfulness, grounding the individual in the present moment. Similarly, practicing mindfulness during mundane tasks, such as washing dishes or taking a walk, encourages a state of calm and appreciation for the present.

Building a regular mindfulness practice requires consistency and patience. Setting aside even a few minutes each day for meditation, mindful breathing, or reflection can lead to significant improvements in emotional stability and overall well-being. Using guided mindfulness apps or joining a local meditation group can also provide support and structure for those new to the practice. With time, mindfulness becomes a natural part of daily life, offering a steady foundation for navigating emotional challenges with grace and resilience.

Incorporating mindfulness into decision-making processes further highlights its transformative impact. By pausing to assess the emotions and thoughts underlying a decision, individuals can make choices that align with their values and long-term goals. This reflective approach minimizes impulsive actions driven by fleeting emotions, fostering a sense of intentionality and purpose. For instance, before responding to an upsetting email, taking a mindful pause can help craft a thoughtful reply that reduces tension and promotes understanding.

Mindfulness also enhances resilience by shifting focus away from uncontrollable external circumstances and toward internal resources. This inward focus empowers individuals to handle setbacks with adaptability and strength. By acknowledging emotions without being consumed by them, mindfulness helps cultivate a balanced perspective, enabling individuals to persevere through difficulties without losing sight of their inner calm.

Through consistent practice, mindfulness creates a ripple effect that touches every aspect of life. It equips individuals with the tools to approach challenges with emotional steadiness, fosters deeper self-awareness, and enhances the quality of interactions with others. By committing to mindfulness, individuals can cultivate a lasting sense of peace and emotional stability, providing a foundation for meaningful personal growth and fulfillment.

Building Resilience Through Self-Reflection and Growth

Emotional resilience is the ability to recover from adversity while maintaining a sense of emotional stability and well-being. It is not about avoiding challenges but about facing them with adaptability, courage, and inner strength. This quality allows individuals to remain grounded in difficult situations, learn from experiences, and emerge with greater emotional depth. Resilience is essential because life often presents unpredictable challenges, and the capacity to respond constructively ensures personal growth rather than stagnation or regression. Cultivating resilience builds a foundation for long-term mental and emotional health, equipping individuals with tools to handle change, loss, or uncertainty.

Journaling serves as a powerful method to foster resilience by providing a safe space for self-reflection. Writing down thoughts and emotions enables individuals to process experiences and gain clarity about their internal world. Through consistent journaling, patterns in reactions, triggers, and coping mechanisms can be identified, helping individuals better understand their strengths and areas for improvement. For example, after a difficult interaction, writing about the event allows one to analyze emotional responses and consider alternative ways of handling similar situations in the future. This process promotes self-awareness and empowers individuals to approach challenges with confidence.

Therapy is another valuable avenue for building resilience. Working with a professional creates an environment where individuals can explore emotions, identify limiting beliefs, and develop strategies for overcoming obstacles. Therapy often provides tools for reframing negative thoughts, enabling individuals to view setbacks as opportunities for growth rather than insurmountable barriers. A therapist can guide clients in setting realistic goals, managing stress, and strengthening their emotional foundations. This collaborative approach fosters empowerment, helping individuals feel equipped to face life's difficulties with renewed determination.

Turning setbacks into opportunities requires a shift in perspective and deliberate action. Resilient individuals recognize that challenges often come with lessons that can be harnessed for personal development. For instance, a professional failure might lead to discovering a new passion or skill set that aligns more closely with long-term aspirations. Reframing adversity as a stepping stone rather than an obstacle transforms moments of struggle into meaningful growth. This mindset encourages proactive problem-solving and helps individuals move forward with purpose.

One effective strategy for cultivating resilience is practicing gratitude. Focusing on positive aspects of life, even during tough times, shifts attention away from what is lacking and toward what is abundant. Keeping a gratitude journal, where three things to be thankful for are recorded daily, can rewire the brain to focus on the good, fostering a sense of hope and resilience. This practice not only enhances emotional well-being but also builds a reservoir of positivity to draw upon during challenging moments.

Building resilience also involves setting achievable goals and celebrating progress. By breaking larger challenges into smaller, manageable steps, individuals can maintain motivation and track their accomplishments. This approach reinforces a sense of control and reduces feelings of overwhelm. For example, someone recovering from a personal loss might focus on rebuilding daily routines or reconnecting with supportive friends, gradually restoring a sense of normalcy. Celebrating small victories along the way bolsters confidence and reinforces the belief that growth is possible, even after setbacks.

Mindful reflection is another tool for resilience. Taking time to pause and evaluate experiences encourages a deeper understanding of emotions and behaviors. For instance, after overcoming a difficult situation, reflecting on what strategies were effective and what could be improved strengthens the ability to handle future challenges. Mindful reflection fosters self-compassion, allowing individuals to acknowledge their efforts and recognize that setbacks are a natural part of life's journey. This practice reduces self-criticism and builds emotional fortitude.

Resilience is further enhanced by cultivating supportive relationships. Connecting with others who provide encouragement and understanding creates a sense of belonging and safety. Sharing experiences with trusted individuals offers new perspectives and reminds individuals that they are not alone in their struggles. Seeking out mentors or role models who have successfully navigated similar challenges can inspire confidence and provide practical guidance for overcoming obstacles.

Engaging in physical activities also contributes to resilience. Regular exercise improves mood, reduces stress, and strengthens the mind-body connection. Activities such as yoga, running, or even walking outdoors promote mental clarity and emotional stability. Physical movement releases endorphins, enhancing overall well-being and providing a natural counterbalance to emotional strain. Incorporating physical activity into daily routines creates a strong foundation for resilience by improving both physical and emotional health.

Developing resilience requires patience and consistency. It is not a quality that appears overnight but rather one that grows through intentional practices and a commitment to self-improvement. Embracing challenges as opportunities to learn and grow cultivates a mindset that thrives under pressure. Over time, these practices create a resilient foundation that supports emotional stability, enabling individuals to face adversity with confidence and strength.

Coping Strategies for Overcoming Emotional Setbacks

Emotional setbacks come in many forms, including loss, betrayal, failure, or sudden changes in life circumstances. Such experiences often disrupt emotional equilibrium, leading to feelings of despair, frustration, or uncertainty. The process of coping begins with acknowledging these emotions without judgment, recognizing them as natural responses to challenging situations. Denial or suppression often delays healing, while acceptance opens the door to constructive action. Identifying the specific source of distress provides clarity and helps in developing tailored strategies for recovery.

Support systems play a critical role in navigating emotional setbacks. Trusted friends, family members, or mentors provide validation, comfort, and guidance during difficult times. Their presence fosters a sense of belonging and reminds individuals that they do not have to face challenges in isolation. Openly sharing emotions within these supportive relationships can ease the weight of burdens and allow for fresh perspectives. Professional support, such as counseling or therapy, offers additional tools to process emotions and develop effective coping mechanisms. Therapists provide a safe space for exploring feelings and identifying actionable steps toward emotional resilience.

Bouncing back from setbacks requires cultivating self-awareness and adopting proactive strategies. Mindfulness techniques, such as focusing on the present moment, help ground individuals in reality rather than allowing them to dwell excessively on the past or worry about the future. Deep breathing, body scans, or mindful meditation calm the nervous system, promoting clarity and reducing emotional overwhelm. These practices enable individuals to approach challenges with a clear mind, increasing the likelihood of finding effective solutions.

Creating a structured approach to recovery enhances emotional stability. Establishing a daily routine that includes self-care activities such as exercise, healthy eating, and adequate sleep reinforces a sense of control and well-being. Physical activity releases endorphins, lifting mood and reducing stress. Consistent sleep patterns and balanced nutrition provide the energy needed to tackle emotional challenges with resilience. By prioritizing these habits, individuals build a strong foundation for recovery and prevent further emotional strain.

Reflecting on past experiences is another valuable tool for overcoming emotional setbacks. Journaling offers a way to process thoughts and emotions, helping individuals identify patterns in their responses to challenges. Writing about feelings not only releases pent-up tension but also provides insight into areas where growth is possible. Reviewing journal entries over time reveals progress and reinforces the understanding that setbacks, while painful, are often temporary. Through reflection, individuals gain clarity and strength to move forward with purpose.

Developing a sense of gratitude during difficult times may seem counterintuitive, but it can significantly enhance emotional resilience. Shifting focus to aspects of life that remain positive fosters a sense of hope and diminishes feelings of helplessness. Keeping a daily list of things to be thankful for trains the mind to recognize joy even amidst challenges. Gratitude does not diminish the validity of pain but creates a balance that supports emotional recovery. This perspective empowers individuals to rebuild their lives with optimism and determination.

Setting small, achievable goals is essential when overcoming setbacks. Breaking larger challenges into manageable steps provides a sense of accomplishment and keeps progress within reach. For example, someone coping with career failure might begin by updating their skills, networking, or pursuing new opportunities. These incremental efforts restore confidence and demonstrate that moving forward is possible. Celebrating small wins along the way reinforces motivation and builds momentum toward greater achievements.

Maintaining emotional stability also involves learning to communicate needs effectively. During times of distress, clearly expressing emotions and seeking support from loved ones creates an environment of understanding and empathy. Conversations grounded in honesty and respect strengthen relationships and provide reassurance. This open exchange fosters mutual trust, allowing both parties to support one another through challenges. Effective communication transforms setbacks into opportunities for connection and collaboration.

Resilience often requires reframing negative experiences into opportunities for growth. While setbacks are undeniably painful, they also offer lessons that contribute to personal development. Reflecting on what went wrong and considering alternative approaches for the future shifts focus from blame to constructive action. This mindset encourages adaptability, creativity, and problem-solving, all of which are essential for navigating life's complexities. By embracing change and viewing challenges as catalysts for improvement, individuals emerge stronger and more prepared for future obstacles.

Incorporating creative outlets into the coping process provides an additional avenue for healing. Activities such as painting, writing, or playing music allow for emotional expression that may be difficult to articulate through words alone. These outlets channel emotions into something tangible, offering relief and fostering a sense of accomplishment. Creative endeavors also stimulate the mind, promoting innovative thinking and a broader perspective on challenges. Engaging in such activities supports emotional recovery while nurturing the soul.

Finally, learning to let go of perfectionism is key to overcoming setbacks. Striving for unattainable standards often leads to self-criticism and emotional exhaustion. Accepting that mistakes and imperfections are part of the human experience fosters self-compassion and eases the pressure to perform flawlessly. This mindset creates space for growth and encourages individuals to focus on progress rather than perfection. By practicing self-kindness, individuals build emotional resilience and the confidence to face life's inevitable ups and downs.

Coping with emotional setbacks is a deeply personal journey, but the strategies outlined here offer a roadmap for recovery. Through mindfulness, support systems, structured routines, and self-reflection, individuals can navigate challenges with grace and determination. By embracing setbacks as opportunities for growth, they cultivate resilience and develop the tools necessary to thrive in the face of adversity. Each step taken, no matter how small, contributes to a stronger, more balanced emotional foundation.

Self-Reflective Questions

1. What are the situations or triggers that most often cause me to feel emotionally unbalanced, and how do I typically respond to them?

2. When was the last time I felt fully present in a moment, and what contributed to that sense of awareness?

3. How do my thoughts and emotions influence the decisions I make during challenging times?

4. What practices or habits currently help me regain stability when life feels overwhelming, and are there areas I could improve?

5. How does my perception of a setback shape my emotional response and ability to recover?

Transformative Exercises

1. Breath Observation Practice:

Dedicate ten minutes daily to focusing solely on your breath. Notice its rhythm, depth, and sensation. Each time your mind wanders, gently bring it back to your breathing. This fosters a sense of calm and reinforces emotional steadiness.

2. Resilience Reflection Journal:

At the end of each day, write about one challenge you encountered and how you managed your emotions. Reflect on what worked, what didn't, and what you might do differently next time. This builds self-awareness and fosters growth.

3. **Mindful Gratitude Walk**:

Take a 15-minute walk focusing on your surroundings. Observe the sights, sounds, and scents without judgment. Identify three things during your walk that bring you gratitude, reinforcing resilience through appreciation of the present moment.

4. **Resilience Visualization Exercise**:

Close your eyes and picture a past situation where you overcame a difficult challenge. Reflect on the strengths and resources you used. Visualize applying those same qualities to future obstacles, reinforcing confidence in your ability to persevere.

5. **Resilient Action Plan**:

Identify a current stressor and break it into actionable steps. Write each step down and prioritize them. As you tackle each task, acknowledge the progress you are making, reinforcing the habit of steady, mindful action even during adversity.

FREE GIFT

Scan This QR Code To Access The Bonus

Scan Me

CONCLUSION

As you reach the end part of this emotional detachment workbook, it is important to reflect on the transformative journey you have undertaken. The process of learning to detach emotionally, establish boundaries, and prioritize your well-being is not a destination but a continuous evolution. This journey represents your character arc—a proof of your courage, resilience, and willingness to grow. You have confronted old patterns, embraced new perspectives, and taken meaningful steps toward reclaiming your emotional freedom. Each exercise completed and every moment of self-reflection has contributed to a stronger, more grounded version of yourself.

Throughout this workbook, you've explored themes of self-awareness, emotional balance, and resilience. These lessons reinforce the idea that true healing and growth require intentional action and self-compassion. Detachment does not mean disconnection(I believe you know that by now)—it is about creating space for healthier relationships with others and, most importantly, with yourself. By internalizing these principles, you are equipped to face life's challenges with clarity and grace.

Now is the time for action. The tools and strategies you've learned from this book are meant to be applied—not just today, but in the days, weeks, and years ahead. Consider how you can implement these insights in your personal and professional life. Set clear boundaries, communicate assertively, and protect your emotional space. Embrace self-care as a daily practice, not a fleeting indulgence. You can also share what you've learned with others, inspiring those around you to begin their own journeys of growth and healing.

This journey may have brought moments of vulnerability, but it is in those moments that true transformation begins. The emotional impact of this work lies in its ability to empower you to move forward with intention and strength. You are not defined by your past or the challenges you have faced, but by the choices you make moving forward.

Let this book be a definitive step toward a life of emotional clarity and fulfillment. However, leave room for further exploration and continued growth. Healing is a process, and every new day offers an opportunity to deepen your understanding and practice.

As you continue your life, carry with you a renewed sense of purpose and an unwavering belief in your ability to thrive. You have the tools to create a life rooted in peace, authenticity, and balance. The work you've done while engaging with this book is just like the beginning. Your journey continues, and the path ahead is filled with limitless possibilities for growth and freedom.

Workbook For The Ultimate Complex PTSD Healing Journey

Empowering Affirmations For Trauma Recovery

Overcoming Emotional Blackmail: A Gaslighting Recovery Workbook

Beyond Manipulations And Illusion

Your Feedback Matters!

Dear Reader,

Thank you for choosing and allowing this guide to become a part of your journey toward emotional detachment, healing, and personal growth. Writing this book has been both an honor and a privilege, and knowing that it has reached you fills my heart with gratitude and purpose. Your trust in my books inspires me to continue creating resources that empower, uplift, and transform.

Every word in this guide was written with your growth and freedom in mind. It is my deepest hope that the exercises, reflections, and insights have resonated with you in meaningful ways, bringing clarity and progress to areas where you seek change.

As you move forward, I humbly ask for your support in helping others discover this resource. If this guide has been helpful, I would greatly appreciate it if you could leave a positive review. Your words not only inspire me as an author but also provide encouragement to others who may be seeking the same transformation you've experienced.

Please feel free to share this book with someone who might benefit from its insights, or consider gifting a copy to a loved one. Together, we can create ripples of change, fostering healing and growth in lives beyond our own.

Thank you once again for your trust, your time, and your commitment to this journey. May you continue to find strength, clarity, and joy as you embrace the path ahead.

With heartfelt gratitude,
EVELYN T. AVERY

NOTE

NOTE

www.ingramcontent.com/pod-product-compliance
Lightning Source LLC
Chambersburg PA
CBHW040208110726
48005CB00019B/2936